Southern Folk Art

FOLK ART

EDITED BY
CYNTHIA ELYCE
RUBIN

Oxmoor House®

Published by Oxmoor House, Inc.
Book Division of Southern Progress Corporation
P.O. Box 2463, Birmingham, Alabama 35201

Library of Congress Catalog Number: 84-61210
ISBN: 0-8487-0645-5
Manufactured in the United States of America

First Edition

Editor-in-Chief: John Logue
Editors: Rebecca Brennan, Cecilia C. Robinson
Editorial Assistants: Pamela Hall, Lisa Gant, Susanna Rogers
Production: Jerry Higdon, Rick Litton, Jane Bonds
Art Director: Bob Nance

Contents

Grave marker, Charles Decker.

Foreword

Today it is customary to speak of the "discovery" some seventy years ago of American folk art by artists and antiquarians who began to collect such diverse objects as portraits by then unknown limners; primitive landscapes and naive watercolors; examples of American folk sculpture, including weather vanes, shop signs, and decoys; and painted and decorated furniture. These simple and unpretentious reminders of an earlier America appealed to a generation of artists who in their own work were experimenting with simplified design, distorted perspective, and bold color. About the same time, differing interests reflecting a similar exploration for roots prompted the descendants of Pennsylvania German pioneers of the eighteenth and early nineteenth centuries to begin the collection and documentation of their own folk heritage. In this manner, a "school of American folk art" began to have its early definition.

This interest, however, was confined almost wholly to the northeastern United States. As a result, the pioneering publications and museum catalogs in the field of American folk art are concerned primarily with one

Front yard of the Henry Schaffner–Daniel Krause Pottery in Salem, North Carolina.

VII

Alkaline-glazed jug, northeastern Alabama.

geographic area. Building upon this earlier work, a substantial body of literature has evolved concerning the folk heritage of the Northeast. The problem, of course, is that this literature often suggests that it is representative of the entire nation; little attention has been given to the rich and diverse tradition of folk art in the American South. This is ironic, perhaps, for while the South has received little attention in folk art circles, it has engendered intensive interest by folklorists who have found an impressive body of material to record in the songs, folkways, and uninterrupted craft traditions of the people. Until recently, however, little attention was given to Southern folk art as an expression of artistic sensibilities. For too long its aesthetic merits have gone unacknowledged. This bias may be historical in nature; curators and collectors simply became accustomed to looking at the more familiar northeastern artistic traditions.

The last decade has seen a recognition of the South's heritage in folk art. Detailed examinations have been undertaken of Southern textiles, especially quilts, in several outstanding regional and statewide exhibitions. Afro-American folk traditions in Southern crafts have been carefully examined; the specialized exhibitions and publications of several Southern museums, although not primarily concerned with folk art, have included important discoveries in such areas as Virginia and North Carolina Fraktur; considerable work has been done on Southern pottery; and my own work, *Folk Painters of America*, included a broad look at the Southern folk painting tradition. Notwithstanding the increase in scholarship, there has been no comprehensive overview of Southern folk art from an art historical perspective. This book and the exhibition which it accompanies provide the first opportunity to see in full context the folk art of the American South.

In preparing for this book and exhibition, Cynthia Elyce Rubin undertook a long, diligent, and intensive search throughout all the Southern states, a prodigious feat in itself. Not only was she faced with an immense geographic area, but even more importantly, with extraordinary diverse cultural and ethnic patterns. The South is not monolithic; on the contrary, the Cajuns of Louisiana, the Moravians of North Carolina, the Germans of Texas, the Spanish of Mobile, Natchez, and Florida, the mountain people of Appalachia, and those who have maintained the wonderful Afro-American

Interior of Burlon Craig's kiln.

Water cooler, Thomas Chandler.

IX

Decker's Keystone Pottery.

tradition—just a few of the many groups whose folk art has enriched the South—have all contributed towards the creation of an original and unique heritage that claims connections with a complex, intriguing past. Cynthia Rubin is to be congratulated for assuming this task and for persevering and succeeding in her effort.

Robert Bishop
Museum of American Folk Art

Portrait of Ann Elizabeth Quarles.

Introduction

The seeds for this Southern folk art exhibition and book were planted in the summer of 1981 when, as a student at the Institute of the Museum of Early Southern Decorative Arts in Winston-Salem, North Carolina, I learned for the first time about Southern backcountry living.

I was privileged to visit potter Burlon Craig of Lincoln County, North Carolina, and with fascination I watched him ply his trade on the treadle wheel. In the old, time-honored tradition, he continues to produce alkaline-glazed stoneware in his authentic groundhog kiln, using the materials and methods of his predecessors. On that same hot summer day, I also met Minnie Reinhardt, the painter known as "Cawtawba Valley's Grandma Moses," a woman of great charm and wit, who led me through her home while describing the "memory" pictures on the walls.

Those visits were the catalyst for what has become my full-time avocation; I searched for the books and articles on the folk art of the South, only to find that there were few written. Believing the whole subject would make an intriguing exhibition, I wrote a preliminary proposal and submitted it to the Museum of American Folk Art.

Alkaline-glazed stoneware, northeastern Alabama.

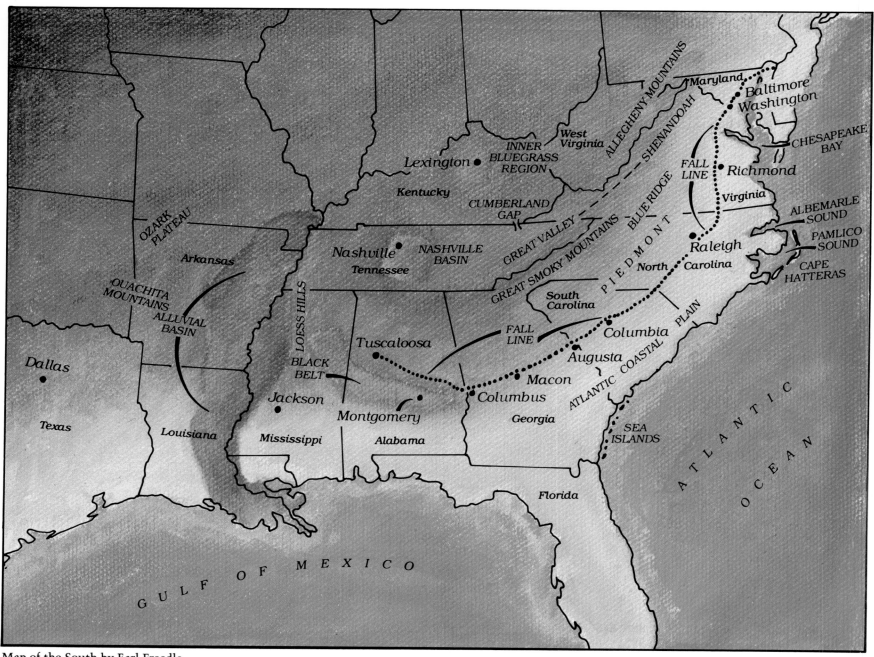

Map of the South by Earl Freedle.

ALKALINE-GLAZED STONEWARE CENTERS

1 Edgefield District (Aiken, Edgefield, Greenwood counties), South Carolina.
2 Catawba Valley (Catawba, Lincoln counties), North Carolina.
3 Eastern Crawford County, Georgia.
4 Mossy Creek District (White County), Georgia.
5 Randolph County, Alabama.
6 Rusk County, Texas.

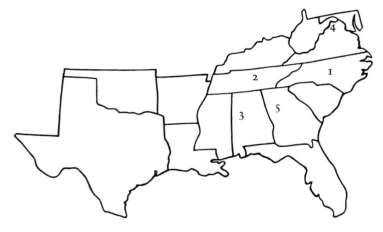

SALT-GLAZED STONEWARE CENTERS

1 Eastern Piedmont (Chatham, Moore, Randolph counties), North Carolina.
2 Middle Tennessee (De Kalb, Putnam, White counties).
3 Northwest Alabama (Lamar, Marion, Tuscaloosa counties).
4 Valley of Virginia (Strasburg).
5 Atlanta (Fulton County) and Jugtown (Pike, Upson counties), Georgia.

EARTHENWARE CENTERS

1 Moravian communities (Forsyth County), North Carolina.
2 Piedmont (Guilford, Lincoln, Randolph, Rowan counties), North Carolina.
3 Great Road (southwestern Virginia and eastern Tennessee).
4 Valley of Virginia (Strasburg, Winchester).

XIII

Detail from sampler, North Carolina.

Owl by Edgar Alexander McKillop.

There Dr. Robert Bishop encouraged me to pursue my research for the project. Today, some three years later, I know that I have only scratched the surface. What I have discovered is that the study of Southern folk art has only just begun. In the past, the emphasis of investigation into American decorative arts has been overwhelmingly on the heavily urbanized Northern states. Until this last decade, many scholars would have us believe that few arts worthy of mention exist south of Baltimore, but we are becoming more and more aware that this is just not so.

Public consciousness has been raised in several ways. Two influential events were the nation's Bicentennial celebrations and the *Foxfire* project of collecting folklore, which began in a Georgia school and whose success was a publishing phenomenon. And, of course, the Museum of Early Southern Decorative Arts has been a leader in locating, cataloging, and preserving Southern folk art through its surveys of the South and in helping Southern states to initiate surveys of their own.

Clearly, interest has been sparked, and out of this increasing attention, the Southern folk artist is being taken from the realm of the unschooled itinerant to that of the recorder of history, essential to further understanding of our culture and national heritage.

However, the South does not easily yield its cultural harvest. With the exception of a few cities, such as Charleston, Savannah, Baltimore, and New Orleans, the early South was a predominately agricultural area. The sophistication of Tidewater aristocrats bore little resemblance to the simple ways of the backcountry farmers. Primitive roads, struggle for survival, and low population density perpetuated rural, cultural, and artistic isolation.

The backcountry folk came from diverse ethnic stocks. They immigrated from England, France, the Canadian province of Acadia, Scotland, Ireland, Wales, the German cantons of Switzerland, and Germany, and they spoke English, French, German, and local dialects. Instead of adopting an English culture adapted to the American environment, they evolved their own distinctive life-styles and artistic expressions based on their "old country" traditions and influenced by the various physical aspects of the areas that they settled.

Termed *folk art*, these artistic expressions were created outside the

European academic tradition. Often called "naive" or "primitive," the works encompass an endless variety of forms and materials: coverlets, quilts, portraits, landscapes, advertising signs, pots, tables, and chairs, to name just a few. Certain visual characteristics can often distinguish types of folk art. For instance, most folk painting is characterized by flattened two-dimensional forms in crisp outlines and great attention to decorative detail. There is a lack of perspective or lifelike modeling. While folk art does not show perfect technical mastery, its creator, working in his rural setting, understood effective use of color, pattern, and line. In furniture, this was often translated into a stylistic time lag. Older styles would be mixed with newer taste. Today, the combination seems pleasing and eccentric.

Folk art often related to popular culture embodying forms and motifs from everyday living. Some folk artists were craftsmen with an aesthetic bent; others were self-taught professionals. Most made only a portion of their livings from art; house and sign painters painted portraits; blacksmiths fashioned artistic andirons; stonecutters made sculpture. Art is a creative response to the world around the artist, and sensibility to life itself was the source of inspiration for the folk artist. What most had in common was that their works were aesthetically pleasing—alive with vigor and originality and with a strong emphasis on color, rhythm, and design. Folk art's appeal is direct and intimate.

Recent attempts to define folk art have compared it with fine arts. It has been said that the latter moves us through an intellectual process deriving relationships by means of mental understanding; folk art appeals to our emotions. It appeared early in the northeastern section of America with the itinerant limner painting portraits of mid-seventeenth-century citizens. It also is rooted in the cultural context of European handicraft traditions, such as those of the German-speaking Swiss, Alsatian, and German immigrants who produced colorful Fraktur, painted furniture, and carved gravestones, often ornamented with traditional Rhenish symbols: the tulip, the rosette, and the multicolored bird.

Folk art is generally created by artists who have not received professional training and who exhibit a personal, naive quality in their mode of representation. Moreover, their manner of work is not akin to the academic

Detail from portrait of Mary Ann (Battle) Collier and her children.

Geometric design of pen, ink, and watercolor; North Carolina.

View of Natural Bridge, attributed to Virginia.

styles of the times. It is a highly personalized art expression, although it may draw, perhaps even subconsciously, from traditional forms. Works are individual—each an odyssey of personal discovery.

Even though much of the folk art created today is being produced mainly by Southerners, only recently has attention been drawn to the South's rich heritage in traditional folk art. This seems unusual because before the recent "modernization" and popularity of the Sunbelt, the lack of industry and the agricultural focus of the society tended to uphold the long-standing custom of doing things. Southern folk artists were often people just "doing like granddaddy did."

Clearly this landmark exhibition and its accompanying book, *Southern Folk Art,* present an extraordinary array of objects, all fully developed art forms containing that quality of unself-conscious natural beauty that folk art enthusiasts savor. Their diversity, their original forms, and their vitality and color, all connecting them to a rich and bountiful past, are amazing.

Through birth and baptismal certificates, homespun textiles, quilts, furniture, pottery, and the other bits and pieces used in people's daily lives which record the life of a civilization, we bear witness to a South that has largely gone unexplored. *Southern Folk Art* uncovers many pieces formerly tucked away in private collections and begins a whole new era of investigation in folk art scholarship. As we all undoubtedly will look more closely at distinctive regional and cultural characteristics, this exhibition will redefine American artistic expression. It offers an unprecedented opportunity to examine the wide-ranging, little-known world of the Southern heritage.

Too often the South has been pictured as a land of serene white mansions with moonlit gardens and fireflies flickering in humid summer evenings. Far more accurate and thrilling has been its role of change in a rapidly moving world. That the South has changed less and at a slower pace than the North is part of its strength. We who love and appreciate continuity and tradition cherish Southern distinctiveness with its unique character and down-home magic. Its folk art reflects the very soul of the South.

Cynthia Elyce Rubin
Museum of American Folk Art

Bear sculpture, ca. nineteenth century.

Pottery

The Pottery Tradition

Southern folk pottery has begun to receive its proper recognition only in the last decade. By contrast, since the beginning of this century, collectors, curators, and ceramic historians have accumulated and admired the decorated earthenwares and stonewares of New England, the mid-Atlantic states, and, to a lesser extent, the Midwest. A few farsighted souls did gaze southwards where they discovered the bright earthenwares of the Great Valley of Virginia and the Moravian communities of North Carolina. Most, however, were content to dismiss the typical pottery of the South as too crude or primitive or devoid of artistic merit to be worthy of notice. Ironically, a common one-gallon jug that once commanded a dime might now net one hundred dollars—and never be filled with anything!

Perhaps there were good reasons for this neglect. The Southern potter did not live in cities such as Boston, New York, or Philadelphia. Instead, he worked in rural regions, in hamlets with colorful names such as Chucky Valley, Erect, Whynot, Pottersville, Bacon Level, and of course, Jugtown. There his products were much appreciated by a hardy, self-sufficient people who demanded a steady supply of pickle jars, syrup jugs, milk crocks, butter churns, cream pitchers, and baking dishes to sustain them from one year to the next. But few regarded the craft of pottery as singular or deserving of special attention in any way. Moreover, the potter himself rarely bothered to sign his wares and kept almost no written records. And so he worked on in relative obscurity, often handing over his shop to the next generation.

Trade sign for Gottfried Aust.

Pewter cupboard, pottery, decoys, and rifle from North Carolina. Moravian pottery on table.

Burlon Craig turning a four-gallon jar on his treadle wheel.

Burlon Craig draining the thick alkaline glaze from a large jar.

Another impediment to recognition was the relentless utilitarian nature of the Southern tradition. Over long stretches of time, the potters duplicated the same forms because they were both inexpensive and performed well. All of these wares were designed for hard usage around the home and the farm; they were never intended to grace a mantel or to be enshrined in a china cabinet. Accordingly, little energy was spent in decoration or embellishment. In this eminently practical world, pots were valued for their usefulness, not their appearance.

One of the major ironies inherent in the long-standing disregard for Southern pottery is that the folk tradition continues today. Scattered across the South are numerous small shops operated by families who have pursued the craft for the better part of two centuries in some cases. While most of the indigenous potteries have gradually adopted more modern forms, glazes, technologies, and marketing methods, several potters still "turn" and "burn" in the old way. In many respects, it is this living context, this opportunity to observe a now largely anachronistic folk craft, that has led us to explore and appreciate anew the Southern ceramic heritage.

Alkaline-glazed stoneware from Alabama.

Folk Pottery

Folk pottery is, by nature, conservative, regional, and utilitarian. It is conservative, first of all, in that the necessary skills and knowledge were transmitted through an informal oral tradition and by on-the-job imitation with relatively little change. The world of the folk potter was governed by inherited ideas, but these were not restrictive forces as the modern mind might perceive them. Rather, they provided a positive, reinforcing set of attitudes and practices that served to guide each new generation. Today, Southern folk technology is best embodied in the work of Burlon B. Craig, one of the last folk potters in North Carolina. A potter for over half a century, Craig has made few concessions to modernity. He digs his clay by hand

5

from the South Fork of the Catawba River and hauls it back to his shop to weather. Next, he grinds it in his pug mill, essentially a barrel with a set of rotating knives inside it, though now he powers it with his tractor instead of a mule. Inside his shop, he turns a variety of traditional forms on his treadle wheel, rhythmically pumping the flywheel with his left foot as he pulls up the clay with his hands. The ingredients for his alkaline glazes are crushed in a waterpowered trip-hammer mill located in a stream behind his pasture and then ground in a stone glaze mill. Finally, he burns his wares in a long, low, groundhog kiln, a task requiring some ten hours of arduous labor and nearly three cords of pine slabs. As a boy, Craig learned the craft from a neighbor and then worked as a journeyman throughout the Catawba Valley before establishing his own shop at the close of World War II. Like his numerous forebears, he continues to adhere to the earlier practices because they are both familiar and efficient.

Closely linked to this pervasive stability is the intensely regional nature of the pottery. In part, this stems from the use of local materials—clays, glazing ingredients, fuels—which were available for the taking in nearby river bottoms, fields, and forests. Because he lacked both capital and ready transportation, the Southern potter relied on the bounty of nature and knew well how to use the abundant resources around him. Beyond such direct influences from the environment are the more intangible preferences which developed because the rural pottery-making communities remained largely separate and self-contained. Over time, each region developed its own characteristic forms and glazes as the training and abilities of the potters merged with the needs and tastes of their customers. Thus, the sense of place is embedded in every pot. Even a novice collector can discern the salt from the alkaline glaze, while a more seasoned observer can detect more subtle clues to origin in the shade of the clay body on the bottom of the pot or the shape of a turned rim or strap handle. Perhaps the potters themselves realized how redundant it would be to sign every piece. Their "signatures" are there even without their names.

The third characteristic of folk pottery is its well-known utility. Because the pots had to perform some useful function—storing beans, making butter, watering chickens, even marking graves—there was little reason to alter an obviously efficient design. In all, the Southern potter produced a

Churn, attributed to Texas.

Group of Moravian pottery.

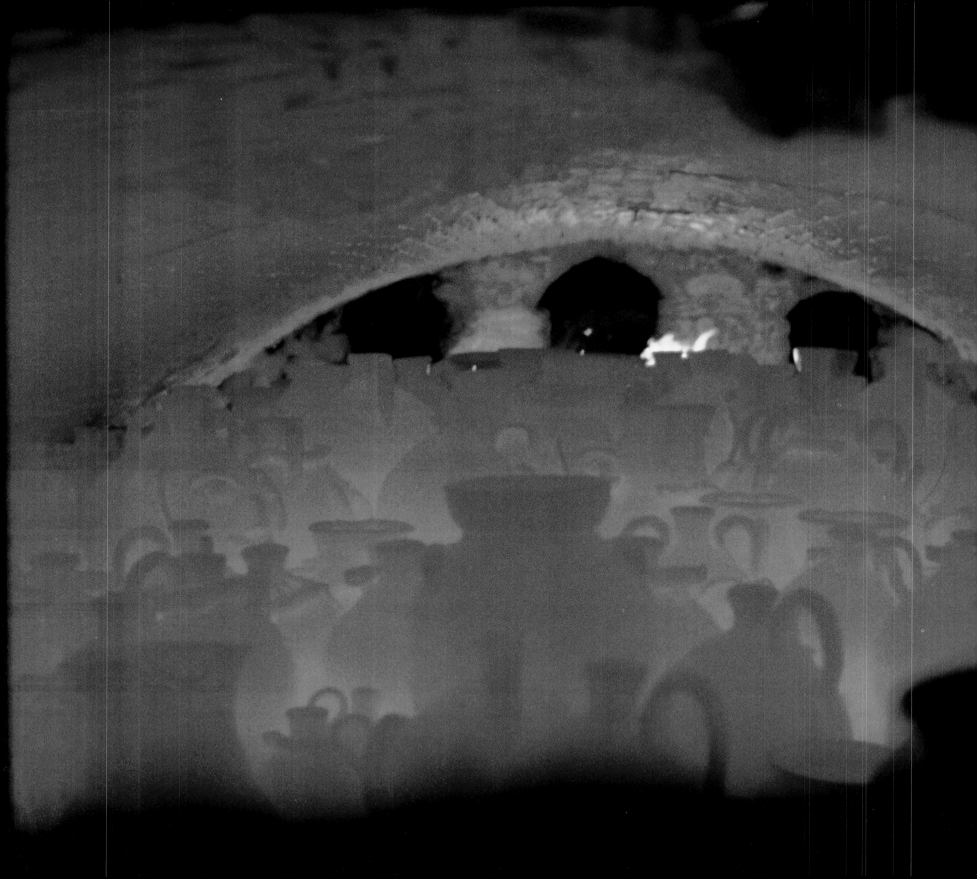

Interior of Burlon Craig's kiln.

Jardiniere, Jacob Jeremiah Eberly.

Storage jar, South Carolina.

9

Churn, South Carolina.

Rundlet, bird/fish potter.

much wider range of forms than is commonly assumed. Too often he is regarded merely as a maker of whiskey jugs for illicit stills or a Snuffy Smith type who was never without a jug of corn liquor balanced on his shoulders. Contrary to this popular stereotype, the potter possessed a varied repertoire of containers, tools, horticultural wares, and even an occasional whimsical creation like a face vessel or an animal. But underlying this diversity was the critical relationship between pottery and food. The bulk of the wares was for the storage, preparation, and consumption of meats, vegetables, fruits, and drinks.

Unquestionably, the preservation of food was the essential function of Southern pottery; well over half of all the pieces ever turned were intended for this purpose. There were just four basic forms for food preservation: the jar, jug, milk crock (pan), and churn. Most important was the jar, the ultimate pottery form and fundamental container that has nourished mankind since his beginnings. Without an ample supply of jars, normally in capacities ranging from one-half to five gallons, a rural family would find it a long, hard winter indeed.

Wares intended for food preparation are far less numerous and may be subdivided into two categories: those used for general preparations, like bowls, strainers, and funnels; and those used for cooking, such as dishes and bean pots. The most common was the simple lead-glazed baking dish or "dirt dish" as it was referred to in some areas. Because earthenware possesses a porous, open body, it better withstands thermal shock than the tight, highly vitreous stoneware and so is more suitable for cooking.

Finally, pots designed for food consumption are even less common. Nineteenth-century inventories reveal that many rural Southern households contained ample quantities of pewter and tin vessels and that the wealthier families also owned ceramic and glass tablewares. Except for the Civil War period when imports were drastically restricted, the local potters found little market for cups, mugs, plates, coffeepots, and teapots. Only the pitcher was found in substantial numbers, in part because it was used for storage as well as serving at meals.

While the major forms of the folk potter's business were closely connected with the local foodways, he also maintained a sideline of implements and horticultural wares. Today, few of the potter's ceramic tools remain in

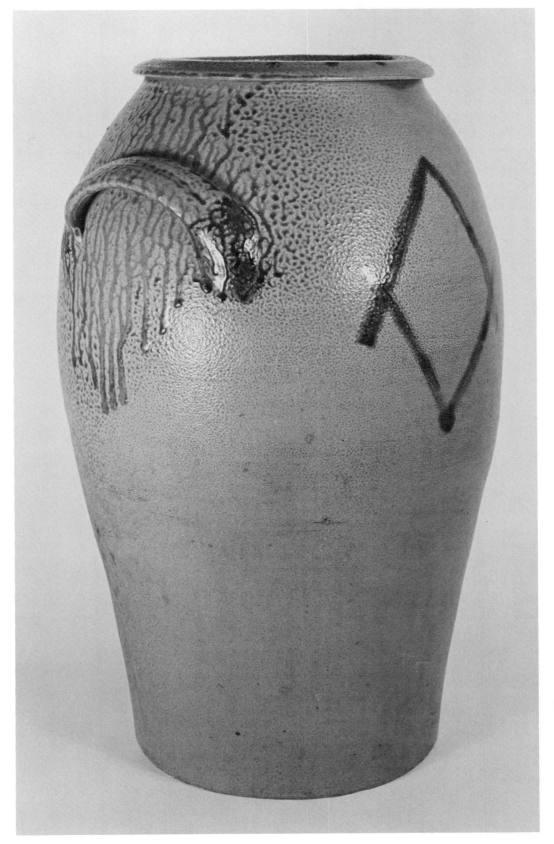

Storage jar,
Edgefield area, South Carolina.

Storage jar, John A. Craven.

11

use, having long since been superseded by more efficient forms or superior materials. There was a time, however, when his grease lamps and candlesticks, chamber pots and banks, birdhouses and chicken waterers, pipes and grave markers were widely used in the home, farm, and community because they were cheap and well served the customers' needs. Within the pragmatic context of folk culture, flowerpots may seem a frivolous production, but solid historical and archaeological evidence reveals that they were in use in Virginia as early as the seventeenth century. Flowers provided an often overlooked aesthetic dimension to rural life, and women enjoyed setting out large numbers of flowerpots along porches or on stepped shelving in the yard. Such arrangements of plants, along with the flower garden itself, constitute an unrecognized form of folk art. As a substantial tourist market developed at the beginning of this century, the potters turned out increasing quantities of vases, urns, and strawberry planters.

Group of Edgefield area pitchers.

Slip-decorated pot with lid, Edgefield District.

"All work and no play make Jack a dull boy" applies to folk potters too. While the potters' world abounded in long hours and exhausting, repetitive labor, they still found time to exercise their sense of play by concocting fanciful forms out of the malleable clay. Such whimsies included miniatures, ring jugs, face vessels, and a variety of sculptured pieces, mostly in human or animal form. Normally these were made at the end of the day or during slack periods when the turner was not filling his shelves with jars and jugs. Often they were intended for a particular person, a member of the family or a close friend, or to commemorate a special occasion, perhaps a holiday or anniversary. Because they were largely nonfunctional and sometimes unique, these forms are very rare. Although least representative of the folk tradition, these novelties are most desired by collectors.

Group of Edgefield area grotesque jugs.

Left: Jar, L. M. Landrum, South Carolina.
Right: Jar, attributed to Amos Landrum.

13

Group of Moravian pottery.

Watch holder, Anthony Baecher.

The period extending from the initial settlement at Jamestown, Virginia, in 1607 to the arrival of the Moravians in central North Carolina in 1753 constitutes what might be termed the "dark ages" of the Southern ceramic tradition. As yet, there are relatively few historical records and archaeological investigations to illuminate developments in this first century and a half. Predictably, excavations at a number of seventeenth-century kiln sites along the James River reveal simple, utilitarian earthenwares reminiscent of the post-medieval styles of rural England. However, at least one potter working at Governor William Berkeley's Green Spring Plantation near Jamestown made some wine cups which emulated the more sophisticated majolica forms current at that time in London. Of much greater complexity is the small factory of the so-called poor potter of Yorktown, which operated roughly from 1720 to 1745 and included numerous buildings and two kilns. Here two new elements are present: a substantial body of salt-glazed stoneware in addition to the lead-glazed earthenware, and clear evidence of the hand of German as well as English potters. But the coastal, or Tidewater, South never developed an extensive ceramic industry. Quality clays were lacking, and the plantation economy necessitated active commerce with England, the West Indies, and the Northeast. Naval stores, foodstuffs, tobacco, and rice were major exports and were exchanged for a variety of manufactured goods including iron, tin, pewter, glass, and ceramic utensils. There was less need here for the native craftsman.

It was in the Piedmont that ideal conditions prevailed for the folk potter: an abundance of fine clay, a rapidly expanding population, an economy dominated by small, self-sufficient farms, and a relative isolation from outside markets. By the middle of the eighteenth century, large numbers of immigrants were wending their way down the Shenandoah Valley of Virginia and then fanning out to the west and south across the Carolinas. Among the early arrivals was a small band of Moravians who, in 1753, began building a fortified settlement called Bethabara on what is now the north side of Winston-Salem. Just two years later, a German potter named Gottfried Aust arrived via Bethlehem, Pennsylvania, constructed a shop and kiln, and commenced selling his wares to settlers all across the Piedmont. Notably, under the guidance of Aust and his successor, Rudolf Christ, the Moravian potteries produced some of the finest earthenwares ever made in the United States. In addition to their graceful, utilitarian pottery, they turned out a large body of slip-decorated wares (slip is a creamlike mixture applied to the outside of the pottery) and press-molded forms. The Moravians differed, in many respects, from the growing numbers of potters scattered across the Southern countryside. They were full-time craftsmen whose skills were perpetuated by the old guild system with its formal ranks of master, journeyman, and apprentice, and until 1829, their business was owned and closely regulated by the community. Moreover, with their penchant for innovation, they cannot simply be labeled folk potters. During the 1770s, the Moravians experimented with sophisticated English creamware and white stoneware, and by the last decade of the century, they were also making German-inspired faience. In fact, few other potters anywhere in eighteenth-century America were so familiar with contemporary European ceramic developments.

The striking achievement of the Moravians has overshadowed the fact that there were many other earthenware potters at work in North Carolina, Virginia, and Tennessee during the late eighteenth and nineteenth centuries. After the Moravians, the most important group of folk potters extended along the Great Philadelphia Wagon Road, which ran from southeastern Pennsylvania down through the center of Virginia. The majority of this group were of German origin, the most prominent being the Bell family, including Peter and his three sons John, Samuel, and Solomon. Working primarily at Winchester and Strasburg, Virginia, the Shenandoah potters produced an enormous variety of utilitarian and decorated earthenwares throughout the nineteenth century. Most characteristic of this region are the highly ornamental forms coated with variegated greens and browns over white. Yet another distinct group of earthenware potters worked along the Great Road, the western extension of the Great Philadelphia Wagon Road that extended from Roanoke through southwestern Virginia and northeastern Tennessee into Kentucky. Many of the storage jars from this area possess a bulbous form with extended, gently curving necks, extruded handles attached only at the terminals, and domed lids, all suggesting that a Moravian

Wall plaque, attributed to John Bell.

Flowerpots; tallest, Solomon Bell; other two, attributed to Jacob Eberly.

17

Pottery plate, ca. 1800s.

Pottery plate, ca. 1850s.

potter may have entered this region around 1800. Finally, at least fifty earthenware potters worked across the North Carolina Piedmont during the late eighteenth and early nineteenth centuries. Their work is unabashedly utilitarian, the most common decorative touch being a hastily applied incised band or wavy combing.

By the first quarter of the nineteenth century, Southern potters and their clientele had begun to recognize the potentially lethal nature of the lead glaze. They also were becoming aware of the rapidly growing stoneware industry in the North. Stoneware possesses several distinct advantages over earthenware. Because it is fired to a much higher temperature, it is far more durable and vitreous. Moreover, it is easier to clean and nontoxic, since no lead is used in the glazing. Two major stoneware traditions evolved in the South. The salt glaze predominates in Virginia, eastern North Carolina, and Tennessee, while the alkaline glaze is found only from the western half of North Carolina south to Florida and west to Texas.

The salt glaze originated in Germany no later than the fifteenth century and gradually spread across Europe into England by the late seventeenth century. Because large quantities of continental and English products were exported to the American colonies, it was not until the early eighteenth century that a native stoneware industry began to develop in the mid-Atlantic region. Aside from isolated occurrences such as the "poor potter of Yorktown" or the Moravians, salt-glazed stoneware was not produced in significant quantities in the South until about 1825. Almost certainly, the largest output occurred in the eastern Piedmont of North Carolina—in particular, Randolph, Chatham, and Moore Counties—where the existence of several hundred potters has been verified. Two large families, the Cravens and the Coles, entered the region in the eighteenth century, and their descendants remain at their wheels today.

Of all the traditional glaze types, salt is least laborious to apply. The potter simply sets his greenware in the kiln, slowly builds the heat to about 2300°F, and then introduces common salt, which vaporizes instantly and covers the exposed surfaces of the wares with a coating of sodium silicate. In North Carolina, the pots were rarely stacked, and the bulk of the salt was introduced through small openings along the top of the arch instead of

18

Jug, Thomas W. Craven.

Storage jar, Thomas W. Craven.

19

Jar, Dave, slave potter.

Jug, Collin Rhodes, Edgefield District.

Grave markers, North Carolina.

through the firebox. Accordingly, the wares often show thick drippings of greenish brown salt and fly ash flowing over the shoulders and sides.

In Virginia, the salt-glaze potters were found in cities such as Alexandria, Richmond, and Petersburg, but the largest single grouping probably occurred in Strasburg in the late nineteenth century. Virginia stoneware differs from that of North Carolina in that it is heavier and more cylindrical; possesses an even, dark gray hue; and is frequently decorated with abstract or floral designs painted on in cobalt blue. The only other state with a substantial output was Tennessee, which was settled somewhat later by families moving south from Pennsylvania and west from Virginia and North Carolina. The majority of potters here employed circular updraft or downdraft kilns, very distinct types from the rectangular, crossdraft groundhog kiln used to the east and south. The greatest number of potters lived in the middle of the state where Andrew LaFever, formerly of Pennsylvania and

Jug, Collin Rhodes.

Water cooler, Tennessee.

Grotesque jug, Mississippi.

Virginia, opened a shop in White County in 1824. Members of the North Carolina Craven family were prominent in western Tennessee, while a German immigrant named Charles Decker opened a large pottery in Washington County in the east in 1872. In addition to the usual utilitarian wares, Decker and his family made face vessels, inkwells, banks, yard ornaments, and grave markers, many of which were decorated with cobalt and incised and molded designs.

Below North Carolina, the salt glaze appears only sporadically. It was used in the Atlanta and Jugtown (Upson and Pike counties) areas of Georgia, in western Alabama (where it was introduced by the Cribbs family from Ohio in the 1820s), and in some parts of Mississippi. The predominant glaze in this lower region is the alkaline glaze, so-called because the flux—either wood ashes or lime—contains compounds of calcium, sodium, and potassium. Truly a homegrown, economical concoction, the potter had only to

21

Advertising ornament, Charles Decker.

add water and an available silica source such as clay, sand, quartz, feldspar, iron cinders, or glass. Today Burlon Craig mixes sifted hardwood ashes, powdered glass, clay, and water and then grinds the solution to a smooth consistency in a hand-powered stone mill.

While the alkaline glaze appears to be of comparatively recent vintage, it is, in fact, an ancient type that predates the salt glaze by more than a millennium. Its origins lie in the Han dynasty (206 B.C.–A.D. 220) of China when the first high temperature kilns were developed to fire stonewares. Subsequently, it spread throughout the Orient where it is still in wide use today, but it was never part of the European ceramic heritage. Just how the technical knowledge of this glaze came to the rural potters of the Carolinas in the early nineteenth century remains a mystery. At present, the most plausible solution is that eighteenth-century European accounts of the Chinese practices made their way into the New World where they may have been read by entrepreneurs like Abner Landrum, who founded the first stoneware pottery in the Edgefield District of South Carolina about 1815. Ultimately, whatever the specific routes of transmission, current research pinpoints two early centers for the evolution of the alkaline glaze: the old Edgefield District (Edgefield, Aiken, and Greenwood counties) and the Catawba Valley (Lincoln and Catawba counties) of North Carolina. From these early centers, migrating potters, such as members of the Leopard and Rushton families, carried the glaze south and west all the way to Texas.

Highly variable in its contents, the alkaline glaze exhibits tremendous diversity in color and texture from one region to the next. For example, when wood ashes are employed as the flux in North Carolina, the glaze tends to be quite dark and thick. In contrast, lime, which was more common in South Carolina and Georgia, produces a smoother, lighter glaze. The potters of the Edgefield District were fortunate to have available clays containing large amounts of sedimentary kaolin. This too produced a paler glaze, which in turn permitted an extensive tradition of slip decoration. But the clays used both in the body of the pot and the glaze will also darken the color if they contain substantial amounts of iron. Potters in the Mossy Creek (White County) section of Georgia added an iron-bearing sand to produce a metallic reddish brown to black hue. Likewise in North Carolina, potters occasionally included small amounts of finely ground limonite or hematite gathered from the fields which resulted in a mottled brown to solid black. For the most part, the typical Southern alkaline glaze was thick, dark, and unpredictable, qualities which hardly allowed for refined or subtle embellishment.

Even with the somewhat limited information presently available, there is clearly an inherent logic underlying the broad patterns of development of Southern folk pottery. The first two centuries constitute an Age of Earthenware, a time during which English and later German forms, glazes, and technologies were transplanted directly into the South. And because of the relative lateness of settlement, little earthenware is encountered below North Carolina. It is easy to forget that Mississippi was not admitted as a state until 1817, Alabama in 1819, and Florida and Texas in 1845. Even before these dates, the more durable stonewares had begun to displace the potentially toxic lead-glazed earthenwares. Moreover, the subsequent distribution of the salt and alkaline glazes makes equally good sense. The salt glaze in the upper South represents a continuation of the Northern tradition, but once across the Virginia–North Carolina border, important changes take place. Cobalt decoration virtually disappears; the groundhog kiln comes into use; and the more typical Southern forms such as the large, bulbous storage jar, the syrup and whiskey jugs, and the milk crock suddenly appear in large numbers. And with these alterations comes the alkaline glaze, which best delineates the native Southern tradition.

Starling Rufus Rogers at the potter's wheel, Georgia.

The Art of the Folk Potter

From an early age, young boys in the South received superb training for their future craft. Working beside the men, they learned to grind and ball the clay, cut the wood, prepare the glazes, and carry seemingly endless quantities of pots in and out of the shop and the kiln. Once into their teens, they commenced turning increasingly complex forms on the treadle wheel, as well as glazing the wares and burning them in the groundhog kiln. And, as they mastered the technical aspects of their trade, they had to respond to the

24

Fifteen-gallon jar, Daniel Seagle.

hard realities of their world. Most importantly, they recognized two major criteria for selling their wares. First, each pot had to hold its stated capacity. Buyers paid by the gallon and wanted to be sure that when they spent a hard-earned fifty cents for a five-gallon jar, they were getting their full money's worth. And next to the proper volume, a smooth, even, well-fired glaze was essential. Both the women who used the wares and the merchants who purchased them in quantity carefully inspected each piece and would reject those on which the glazing was too thin, rough, or underfired. Such pots were difficult to clean and might also leak—in short, they had no value.

Each new generation of folk potters, then, acquired the fundamental wisdom of their forebears; their wares sold if they were useful. Fifty one-gallon jugs from the same kiln all fetched exactly the same price providing, of course, that none was defective. While a purchaser might admire a boldly conceived, carefully trimmed form, he was rarely willing or able to pay more for such extra care. Likewise, the potter knew that there was little point in adding superfluous decoration, in creating "art," when the jar or churn already did what it had to do. Such aesthetic flourishes represented wasted motions, a squandering of time and energy, the potter's most valuable assets. For all such additional efforts in forming, finishing, or embellishing a piece, the potter still received the same standard rate. The net result was that he made less money.

Still, there was beauty in this austere world. In varied, sometimes subtle ways, the potter found the means to go beyond necessity, to transcend the purely functional demands made on his abilities. Sometimes he drew or painted on his pots; less commonly he sculpted them. Most assuredly, he never received the sort of monetary recognition that seems so essential to modern definitions of the value of art. The potter's wares now sell for prices that would have made his head spin.

The most common form of decoration on all types of Southern pottery was simple incising. Before cutting a moist form off the wheel, the potter might use the edge of his trimming chip, his fingernail, a sharp piece of wood, even a fork or comb to cut one or more bands in the neck, shoulder, or belly of the pot. The prime virtue of this technique was speed; one or two

"Great Road" pottery, northeastern Tennessee.

25

Kerosene jug, E. E. MacPherson, Alabama.

rotations of the wheel and the job was done. Such rings helped to accentuate the different sections of a pot and also served to catch the thicker stoneware glazes, most notably the alkaline, thus producing a series of darker bands where the glaze has filled in the grooves. A closely related technique is rouletting, whereby the potter rotated a small wheel on the slowly turning pot. Such coggle wheels were mounted on short, wooden handles and made of both metal and wood. The former were fabricated from small gears or pennies which were filed and pointed and produced a continuous band of dashes. In the eastern Piedmont of North Carolina, these were used to inscribe the gallon capacity; sometimes the potter went further and added a design. The wooden coggle wheel was wider and carved in geometric or floral patterns which were repeated as the potter moved the wheel around the pot. Finally, the potters sometimes acquired small stamps which they pressed into the wet clay. Most were used to mark the gallonage or maker's name, but some left fanciful stars or flowers or even the Masonic compass and square.

Freehand pictorial incising is extremely rare in the South, as it required not only considerable time but also the skill of a draftsman. Occasionally a potter felt the urge to draw a human or animal likeness, but the results were usually quite crude. One remarkable example found in Crawford County, Georgia, is a two-gallon, alkaline-glazed jug made by John C. Avera in 1871. Around the belly of the jug runs a sleek fox pursued by two lean hounds and a hunter with his rifle in hand. An elaborate inscription reveals that this was a presentation piece made for a wealthy neighbor who loved the chase. Outside of such one-of-a-kind efforts, which tend to possess a flat, textureless, cartoonish quality, there is only one extensive body of pictorial incising. About two dozen pieces of salt-glazed stoneware have emerged in the eastern Piedmont of North Carolina which are covered with birds, fish, trees, branches, flowers, Masonic emblems, and varied geometric embellishments. All are skillfully executed, with meticulous feathers and scaling on the birds and fish and elaborate incising on the foliage, handles, and cartouches. Remarkably, none is signed, but nine are dated from 1842 to 1879. Recent research suggests that the creators of these striking wares were members of the Webster family—brothers Edward, Chester, and possibly Timothy—who migrated from Hartford, Connecticut, to Fayetteville, North Carolina, about

1820 and later moved westward into Randolph County, the heart of the salt-glaze industry. Thus, these "bird/fish" pots—jars, jugs, pitchers, an inkwell, and a rundlet—reflect an earlier New England decorative tradition that, long after incising ceased in the North, continued on in the rural South.

Just as he drew, the folk potter also "painted" on his wares, employing the limited palette of colors available to him through his standard glazes. Because it is fired to a relatively low temperature of 1800°F or so, the lead glaze offers a greater range of chromatic possibilities. Both the Moravians and the potters of the Shenandoah Valley often dipped their pots first in a white engobe (a mixture of clay and water) in order to establish a light, contrasting background for their artwork. Most of the other potters, however, simply used the natural yellow, orange, or red of the clay body as their canvas. In addition to the basic white (kaolin) and red (earthenware clay), the potters used well-ground metallic oxides to create green (copper oxide), brown to black (iron oxide), and brown to purple (manganese dioxide). In Virginia, both in the Valley and along the Great Road to the southwest, the potters preferred the simpler technique of spattering the colors in random patterns on the walls of the pot. In contrast, the Moravians created precise geometric and floral patterns, often in three or four colors, by trailing on thick lines of slip from a small clay bottle with a quill in the spout called a slip cup. All of these techniques were common to other areas of the country as well.

With the advent of stoneware, the potters were challenged to find new colors and contrasts because most of the familiar metallic oxides used on the earthenwares would burn off at high temperatures. And here, although their resources were limited, Southern potters devised a number of clever solutions. Like their Northern counterparts, potters in Virginia painted on dark-blue designs using cobalt oxide. Farther south, however, cobalt was used only infrequently and then largely to accentuate rims, handles, incising, or lettering. The few attempts to paint flora or fauna appear crude when compared to the Northern pottery, but it must be emphasized that there were no professional decorators here, nor did the competition warrant such touches. During the late nineteenth century, potters began importing Albany slip, thus adding a smooth, chocolate brown hue to many of their wares. In North

Jug, bird/fish potter.

27

Carolina, Georgia, and Alabama, some potters salt-glazed pieces which had been dipped in slip and achieved a mustard yellow to deep green, appropriately labeled "frogskin" in North Carolina. Because there was no practical need to employ both glazes together since each functioned well alone, it would appear that the potters did so for aesthetic reasons.

Without question, the most original and dramatically embellished Southern stoneware was produced in the Edgefield District of South Carolina, where, during the mid-nineteenth century, Collin Rhodes, Thomas M. Chandler, and others created elaborate slip designs under their alkaline glazes. Kaolin and iron were used to produce two basic light and dark slips which were both trailed and brushed on in swags; tassels; curlicues; floral patterns; fantastically concocted numbers and names; and likenesses of roosters, snakes, pigs, and ladies in billowing hoop skirts. Many Afro-Americans worked in the potteries of this region—the shops were often part of a larger plantation system—and it is possible that some of them, women in particular, played a role in this decorative tradition. In all, the Edgefield pottery is unique in that it appears to combine slip techniques normally used on earthenwares with a stoneware glaze.

Elsewhere in the South, potters devised simpler means of varying their alkaline glazes. The previously discussed use of iron additives in North Carolina and Georgia represents one such option. In the Catawba Valley, early potters such as Daniel Seagle and David Hartzog established the practice of balancing shards of glass across the mouths and handles of pots that had just been set in the kiln. When fired, the glass flowed down the sides in wide, gray to milky white streaks, creating a sharp contrast to the darker glaze. And in northeastern Alabama, at least one potter double-dipped the upper half of some of his pots to achieve a two-toned alkaline glaze.

Only rarely did the potter turn sculptor and create three-dimensional ornamentation. And when he did so, he usually added on to one of his standard utilitarian forms which he first turned on the wheel. In general, the earthenware potters did the bulk of the modeling. Many in the Shenandoah Valley were skilled at making small molds of animals, birds, fish, flowers, leaves, even human forms, and then applying them to the surfaces of pitchers, coolers, bowls, vases, and flowerpots. Combined with the bright, multicolored glazes of the area, they give the wares an unusually busy, rococo

Bowl from washbowl set, attributed to Jacob Eberly.

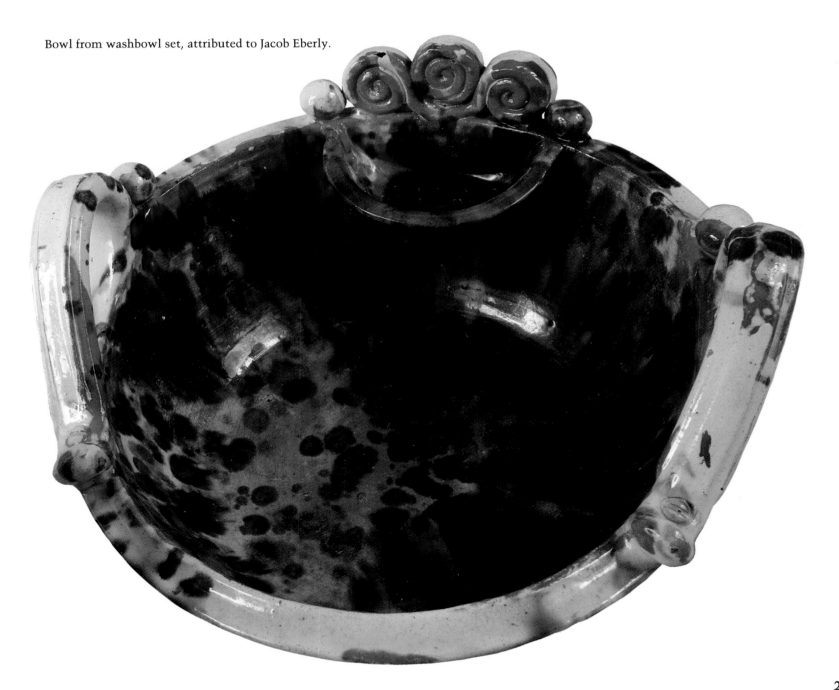

Jar, Robert Mathis, Edgefield District.

Pitcher from washbowl set, attributed to Jacob Eberly.

quality not found in most Southern pottery. Both the Valley potters and the Moravians also molded whole pieces. The former made pitchers, candle-sticks, flowerpots, picture frames, and animals; the latter were recognized for their stove tiles, Bundt pans, toys, and bottles in the forms of fish, chickens, turtles, squirrels, and other small animals. Handmade, freely sculpted pieces are extremely rare, even in the florid Virginia tradition. Among the prominent surviving examples are a pair of log cabins made at the Eberly Pottery to commemorate a Civil War battle; several human fig-ures; and a series of animals, the most renowned being the Bell lions with their zipper mouths, spaghetti-like manes, and upcurled tails. Once again, these were presentation pieces, made specifically for members of the Bell family.

The stoneware potters, by contrast, were far more restrained. Of ex-treme rarity is a large, alkaline-glazed storage jar covered with sprig-molded decorations and attributed to James Long of eastern Crawford County, Geor-gia. Probably made in the 1830s or early 1840s, it features a haloed likeness of Thomas Jefferson and Andrew Jackson on each side. A political advertise-ment for the young Democratic party as well as a sturdy container, this ebullient creation sports applied leaf-and-grape clusters, floral sprays, and two eagles with banners emblazoned HURAH FOR JEFFERSON and HURAH FOR JACKSON. For most stoneware potters, however, the princi-pal sculptural forms were the flowerpot, the grave marker, and the face ves-sel. Their flowerpots were made of both earthenware and stoneware clays, and they were frequently burned in the cooler areas of the kiln, along the sides and near the chimney, where the glazes would not mature. Some were plain, but most were decorated to some degree with combing, fluted rims, possibly even a rough, knotty tree trunk texture, or applied grapes, cordons, flowers, or leaves. Grave markers were made in both turned and tablet forms; in Alabama, the slab was sometimes set into a cylindrical base. Like the flowerpot, grave markers were objects of contemplation and were often elaborately inscribed and lettered with fluted rims, finials, and sinuous, flar-ing shapes.

Front and back of storage jar, attributed to James Long, Georgia.

Overleaf: Pair of pottery lions, S. Bell and sons, Virginia.
Following page: Pottery lion, John Bell.

Storage jar, Daniel Seagle, North Carolina.

Perhaps no form excites contemporary collectors of ceramics more than the face vessel, often referred to as a "face jug," "ugly jug," or "voodoo jug." Made in the form of jugs, pitchers, and cups by potters across the South, face vessels usually have an alkaline glaze or, more recently, a slip glaze. During the last decade, Lanier Meaders of Georgia and Burlon Craig and the Brown family of North Carolina have sold thousands of the face vessels, but in earlier times they were infrequently produced. Making a face jug is extremely tedious work. Once the jug is turned and allowed to dry slightly, the potter must form and apply at least thirteen pieces of clay to create the typical face: ears (2), eyebrows (2), eyes (6), nose (1), lips (2). Optional features include hair, a moustache, a tongue, a beard, horns, glasses, even warts. Finally, the potter must insert the teeth, usually jagged pieces of commercial whitewares, or, on older vessels, white-burning clays or fragments of rock. At a minimum, such embellishments triple the time needed to complete a single piece. Today, well-heeled collectors willingly pay for the added labor, no doubt because they value the piece as sculpture and not as an unadorned usable jug. In the old South, however, there was little market for these leering, pop-eyed, humanoid creations. Perhaps the potter found them useful for venting unexpressed feelings, or maybe for making fun of a neighbor, but few buyers felt the need for ears, eyes, a nose, and a mouth on their water jugs.

Last Shards

In the main, the Southern potter was not an artist. He was a production potter whose primary concerns were to work at a good clip, make economic use of his local resources, and provide a wide range of utilitarian vessels to rural communities. Like his cotton or tobacco, his pots were a cash crop; they provided extra income to purchase the necessities and possibly a few luxuries of life that he could not make or grow himself. Nor was the Southern potter a full-time craftsman. He was often a farmer and active in one or more other occupations as well. Potting, for him, was a seasonal activity that

Face jug, Burlon Craig, 1980.

Jug, Washington Becham, Georgia.

Pig bank, Norman Smith, Alabama.

Dog figures, attributed to the Bell family.

Dog, attributed to Solomon Bell.

had to dovetail with the natural cycle of planting and harvesting. Even his sales responded to cyclic rhythms. In the spring, people needed to replace the churns and milk crocks broken over the winter; in the fall, they required additional jugs and jars to put up their crops. Ultimately, the Southern potter was not a specialist. He was a jack-of-all-trades who mastered the knowledge and skills to execute all phases of his craft along with additional occupations. Thus, it is misleading to compare his wares to the assembly-line products of the factory or the carefully wrought forms of the artist-potter. The Southern potter was a generalist—he had to be—and his work reflects this simple fact.

There were potters, though, who transcended this rigorous world and infused their creations with an extra beauty not demanded by the immediate context. Sometimes they worked in clusters, establishing a more complex and lasting aesthetic tradition as in the Moravian settlements of North Carolina, the Shenandoah Valley of Virginia, and the Edgefield District of South Carolina. At times, one or two individuals recorded their singular mark, as in the "bird/fish" pieces of North Carolina, the fox-hunting jug by John Avera of Georgia, or the two-toned alkaline glazes of an anonymous potter of

Seated whippet, John Bell.

Seated whippet, I. Bell.

northeastern Alabama. With few exceptions, this art was subordinated to function, an integral part of the familiar utilitarian forms.

There is yet another, more subtle level of beauty in these Southern wares. Art need not be self-conscious and controlled. It may reside also in the unadorned and commonplace. True masterpieces lie in the largely undecorated salt- and alkaline-glazed stonewares that are the heart of the Southern pottery tradition. Out of the primitive groundhog kilns where the common clay was seared and transmuted by fire came boldly conceived jars, jugs, churns, and pitchers coated with lustrous, flowing, natural glazes. The product of chance and of human will, these essential forms stir the imagination and evoke admiration for the vision and skills of the unassuming, often anonymous, Southern farmer-potters who created them.

Charles G. Zug III
*The University of North Carolina
at Chapel Hill*

The author gratefully acknowledges the assistance of Howard A. Smith, Associate of Robert M. Hicklin Jr. Inc., in the preparation of this essay.

Zierschrift, Jacob Strickler.

Painting

Folk painting, generally defined as artwork by a nonacademic artist, began to emerge in the Colonial era and peaked in production in the first half of the nineteenth century. For the middle classes, it provided an acceptable substitute for academic art when most Americans were physically and economically isolated from European high culture but desired to emulate the artistic traditions of their respective homelands. The naive and primitive renditions served not only as practical and decorative records of people, landscapes, and events, but also as symbols of upward mobility in the new nation.

Aesthetic merit rather than technical proficiency is the key to folk painting. The images represent an adaptation of the fine arts tradition to prominent outlining, sharpened colors, and simplified, flattened forms. Design is essentially the unifying element, giving each painting its naive appeal.

Many folk artists called themselves limners. Their work proved satisfactory to both rural and urban dwellers alike. Some moved from place to place in search of new commissions, listing their residences at local homes as they traveled. They stayed in each home just long enough to paint portraits of the family members. To take best advantage of the climate, some artists spent their summers in the Northeast and winters in the South.

Portrait of Mrs. C. Billingsly Lomax.

41

Many of these artists had primary careers ranging from medicine and law to sign and house painting. For them, portraiture and landscape painting were simply added sources of income. Although these artists lacked the long, rigorous training of European art academies, they adapted many aspects of artwork to their own specialty. This blending of haphazard education with a craftsman's skills resulted in a unique freedom of expression which we call folk painting.

Folk painters have remained primarily anonymous until recently. The survival rate of nonacademic and academic paintings in the South is less than that of the Northeast due to the destructiveness not only of the Civil War but also the South's high humidity. In fact, it has been estimated that only thirty to forty percent of Southern paintings have survived and less than half of the artists are known. Inadequate information about folk painters is partially the result of the lack of research done in the South. Scattered research material, the expense of traveling long distances, and the fact that a large number of paintings are privately owned have deterred scholars. However, over the past twenty-five years, many artists have been rescued from oblivion by investigative research on the basis of stylistic similarities and an occasional signed piece. Entire artistic identities have been reconstructed through genealogy and in-depth research into period newspapers for advertisements of the arrivals of artists in town.

Southern folk art was primarily produced by untrained artists, but its history mirrors that of Southern academic art. Both painting traditions focus on the people, the quality and quantity of the land, and the changes in Southern society just prior to the Civil War. Folk artists frequently were not Southerners themselves and depicted social conditions from a different, more detached point of view.

The proliferation of folk art began later in the South than in the Northeast. This delay is attributed primarily to slow settlement, an agrarian society, and a small population. As travel was difficult, much of the artists' time was spent traveling from place to place. And needless to say, the Civil War interrupted the artists' work in the South.

Portrait of Mrs. Sophie (Shorter) Lomax.

Memorial picture in watercolor.

Portrait, subject unknown, found in Virginia.

Portrait of Mrs. Keyser.

44

Portrait of Mary Ann (Battle) Collier and her children.

Portrait of Jean Baptiste Wiltz, Louisiana.

Portraiture was the most popular form of Southern painting. It reigned supreme in the late eighteenth and early nineteenth centuries, continuing a well-established academic tradition. Mainly commissioned by the middle and upper classes, portraiture fulfilled a patron's desire to have a copy of his own likeness for posterity. Most patrons could not afford the great academic painters of the day, and many patrons could not distinguish academic from nonacademic art. Portraiture provides an unwritten account of its patrons' aspirations and achievements and reveals their growing sense of identity and national pride.

In addition to the figure itself, the background in portraiture may include details of actual or contrived surroundings and possessions. A column, a scenic view, lace, or jewelry symbolized the actual or intended prosperity of the sitter. Fancy needlework alluded to leisure time. A book in the hand or on a shelf was a symbol of education.

These subtle additions appear in children's portraiture as well. Since both young boys and girls were clothed in dresses, boys were identified by such special accouterments as whips, wagons, books, and dogs, and girls by coral beads, dolls, fruit, and flowers. Children were most often painted individually, though sometimes they were included in family groupings also.

The portrait of Elizabeth Jane Carruthers depicts her at three months old. Born December 29, 1834, in a four-room log cabin in Talladega, Alabama, she survived three husbands and lived to the age of eighty-five. Her painting was found by descendants at the home of her third husband, William S. Chancellor. The artist is unknown.

The "Guilford limner" is a prolific artist who has yet to be identified by name. He painted watercolor portraits in Guilford County, North Carolina, primarily in 1826, 1827, and 1828. His existing thirty-four works include background details surrounding the sitters such as floor cloths, tables, and chairs as well as personal items.

The paintings of John McClintock Logan (1797–1853) and Nancy Dick Patrick Logan (1797–1827) are excellent examples of the Guilford limner's endeavors. Logan immigrated to America from Ireland in 1821. He was an active politician and successful merchant in Greensboro, North Carolina. He married Nancy in 1825, and they soon had their first son, Thomas. Nancy is depicted in mourning for this child which died in infancy. She died in 1827, the same year the portrait was drawn.

Part of the German migration down the Shenandoah Valley included the religious group known as the Moravians who settled in Salem, North Carolina, in 1766. One portrait-and-landscape artist in the sect was Christian Daniel Welfare (1796–1841). Welfare, born in Salem, served the community in many ways, yet his main desire was to be an artist. Welfare went to Philadelphia in 1824; there he studied with Thomas Sully and exhibited his work at the Pennsylvania Academy in 1825. His training may have helped him, but his paintings continued to exhibit a primitive approach. The subjects of Welfare's paintings include religious works, romantic landscapes, and views of Salem.

Portrait of John McClintock Logan.

Portrait of Nancy Dick Patrick Logan.

Portrait of Elizabeth Jane Caruthers.

Portrait of Liza Baker.

Portrait of Sarah Elizabeth Quarles.

Family portraits are rarely found in the South today. Susan Fauntleroy Quarles Nicholson painted her family's (the Quarles) portraits including her sister, brother, and three of his children. Nicholson represents one of the few known Southern female folk artists. Like many folk artists' works, Nicholson's paintings have flat, awkward lines, but they show great detail. She was born in 1804, and it is assumed that she attended an academy in King and Queen County, Virginia, since much of her art reflects schoolgirl motifs. She married Jacob Cannon Nicholson, possibly an artist himself, and in 1839, they advertised "Portrait Painting" in the *Lynchburg Virginian*:

> Mr. & Mrs. Nicholson having taken the house
> formerly occupied by Mr. Bailey, at Amherst Court
> House, are prepared to Paint Miniatures and
> Portraits, for any who may desire it. Our terms
> are moderate, and we invite the public generally,
> and in particular those who are disposed to
> encourage us, to call and examine the quality of
> our Paintings. From the satisfaction heretofore
> given, we hope to meet with liberal encouragement.

Nicholson probably painted the five known portraits of her family during her stay in Lynchburg.

John Drinker was the son of John and Susanna Allen Drinker of Philadelphia, Pennsylvania. His father's occupation as a bricklayer and real estate developer afforded him the means to pursue his painting career. In 1787, Drinker advertised the opening of his first drawing school in the *Pennsylvania Packet*:

> Just opened, A Drawing-School, Upon a New
> Plan . . . Where he intends with the assistance of Mr.
> Pratt, to teach the art of Drawing and
> Colouring . . . Likenesses in
> Miniature, . . . Crayons . . . Oyl [sic] . . . Ornamental
> Painting and Pencil work don [sic] as usual, in oyl or water
> coloures, on wood, tin, copper, glass, ivory, linen or paper.
> Painting on Glass Taught as above, in an elegant and
> durable manner, with or without Metzzotinto [sic] Prints.

Yet Drinker's work in Philadelphia is not well documented.

John Drinker's marriage in 1797 to Elizabeth Peppers of Berkeley County, (now West) Virginia, led to his eventual move to the Shenandoah Valley around 1802. There he painted seven known portraits of prominent citizens of the area.

Jacob Frymire, born between 1765 and 1774, was the son of a Lancaster, Pennsylvania, farmer. Although there is no documentary evidence that he received any instruction in painting, his works show a professional's consistency and quality. By the 1790s, he was well established in his painting

Portrait of Warner Lewis Wormeley.

career, traveling south to Winchester, Alexandria, and Warrenton, Virginia. In 1806, Frymire traveled to Woodford County, Kentucky, where he produced two of his most important portraits—those of General Marquis Calmes IV and his wife, Priscilla Heale Calmes.

Frymire married and resumed residence in Shippensburg, Pennsylvania, by 1810. Living near the Virginia border, he continued to make short trips into that state following new commissions. He is also known to have established a "painting room" at his home where he conducted his portraiture business. With the death of his father in 1816, Frymire started two farms and thereafter ceased to be designated as a painter in the tax listings.

A total of twenty-seven portraits painted by Frymire are known today. The portraits of General and Mrs. Marquis Calmes IV represent his more mature style. The Calmes resided in Woodford County, Kentucky, and were wealthy landowners. General Calmes's education, social status, and wealth are suggested by the book he holds, *T.* [sic] *Life of Dr. B. Franklin.*

Joshua Johnson is the earliest known black portrait artist in America. He is listed in various Baltimore directories of 1796 as a portrait painter among "The free Householders of colour." Little is known about Johnson except that in addition to being a painter, he was a founding member of the First Baptist Church in Washington, D.C., which accepted all men: black, white, free, and slave. His advertisements and listings in Baltimore continued until 1824.

About thirty of Johnson's paintings, mostly from Baltimore between 1795 and 1805, are in existence today. Johnson advertised his skills in the December 19, 1798, edition of the *Baltimore Intelligencer*:

> As a self-taught genius, deriving from nature and industry
> his knowledge of Art: and having experienced many
> insuperable obstacles in the pursuit of his studies; it is
> highly gratifying to him to make assurances of his ability
> to execute all commands, with an effect, and in a style
> which must give satisfaction.

Johnson's work must certainly have been influenced by Charles Peale Polk, since both were working in Baltimore during the 1780s and 1790s.

Portrait of Marquis Calmes IV.

Johnson's subjects are characterized in his portraits by stiff legs, arms, and body; piercing eyes; and a tight mouth.

The works of Charles Peale Polk provide an excellent study in the relationship between the academic and nonacademic artist. Orphaned at an early age, Polk and his two sisters were reared in Philadelphia by their uncle, Charles Willson Peale. Through Peale's influence, the family had a succession of artists, totaling sixteen among the children and grandchildren. Most were taught by Peale himself, whose instructions included copying some of his own works. Polk's first known works are copies of Peale's portraits of George Washington and Comte de Rochambeau which are signed and dated May, 1783.

Polk's life was plagued with financial difficulties, which may have prompted his move to Baltimore in 1791, where there was less competition among portrait painters. In Baltimore he engaged himself in a drawing school and a mercantile business. Still unsuccessful, he and his family moved to Frederick, Maryland, in 1796. From there, he traveled throughout the surrounding counties in Maryland and Virginia seeking commissions. By means of family contacts he continued on to Monticello to paint a portrait of Thomas Jefferson and then moved on to Richmond. Polk became politically active which led to his employment as a government clerk in 1802. He held this position until 1820, but continued to paint portraits as well. Polk's last known portrait is of his third wife, Ellen Ball Downman.

First public documentation of the painter, Frederick Kemmelmeyer, appeared in 1788 in an advertisement in a Baltimore newspaper. He is best known for his paintings of George Washington and Christopher Columbus, although his repertoire includes religious as well as historical paintings. He traveled around the region looking for commissions in Baltimore, Annapolis, and Alexandria. In 1805, Kemmelmeyer moved to western Maryland, where he is known to have painted seven pastel portraits. His last known signed portrait is dated 1816.

With the invention of the daguerreotype in 1839, the market of the folk portrait painter began to diminish. Photography aided the artists by eliminating the need for lengthy portrait sittings, but ironically, many artists eventually abandoned painting for the new art form.

The turn to painting landscapes and historical, genre, and religious

Portrait of the Westwood children, Joshua Johnson.

Portion of wall murals from West Virginia, Reverend Daniel Schroth.

57

Illustration of Martin Luther
from Marburg Hymnal, 1771.

scenes by artists in the nineteenth century reflects the growing sense of identity and pride that Americans had in their towns, farms, and homes. Landscapes were frequently painted from on-site sketches or remembrances, thus their disproportionate appearances. For genre, religious, and historical scenes, however, artists relied heavily on chromolithographs both from this country and abroad. The prints were transformed into paintings by rearranging the composition, simplifying the forms, improvising with the color, and adding a special touch characteristic of the artist. Although copying has a negative connotation as far as folk art is concerned, the effect was usually positive as it broadened the knowledge of these largely self-taught artists.

Two paintings by Frederick Kemmelmeyer serve as examples of the artist's reliance on printed sources. His portrait of Martin Luther is almost a direct copy of the frontispiece from a 1771 version of the Marburg Hymnal. A second example is Kemmelmeyer's famous General George Washington at Fort Cumberland, Maryland. Kemmelmeyer reputedly painted the scene from life. However, the recent discovery of an eighteenth-century German engraving by Daniel Chodowiecki (1726–1801), *The Parade of the Army before Frederick H. at Potsdam*, suggests that this print may have been a source for Kemmelmeyer's work.

Portrait of General George Washington,
Frederick Kemmelmeyer.

Capitol from Market Street, Montgomery, Alabama.

Mother House of the Sisters of Div[ine] Providence and Vicinity, Castroville, Texas, Rudolph Mueller.

60

Battle of New Orleans, Jean Hyacinthe de Laclotte.

Rudolph Mueller (1859–1929) came to the Alsatian community of Castroville, Texas, as a youngster and became the town's shoemaker. Mueller has four known paintings. Two of them, depictions of European castle scenes, are remembered by residents of the area as hanging in the Rehn Saloon, which was frequented by Mueller. The other two paintings are important landscapes of Castroville. They are *Bird's Eye View of Castroville c. 1899*, and *Mother House of the Sisters of Div*[ine] *Providence and Vicinity*. The order was established in 1868, and by 1872, parishioners were building the stone, two-story schoolhouse. To add interest and balance to his painting, Mueller combined this scene with Mt. Gentily, or "Cross Hill," which was actually located several miles away from the Mother House.

Jean Hyacinthe de Laclotte (1766–1829) was originally trained as an architect in France. He immigrated to New Orleans in 1811, and during the War of 1812 was the assistant engineer in the Louisiana army. From sketches executed on the battlefield, he drew a panoramic view of the great battle of 1815. Considered to be the most accurate of all paintings of this scene, Laclotte shows Jackson and his militia on the left behind the Rodriguez Canal with British General Packenham leading his troops in a direct attack from the right. Originally the painting was entitled the *Eighth of January, 1815*, commemorating the date of the Battle of New Orleans, which occurred east of the city on Chalmette Plantation.

An interesting view of Huntsville, Alabama, was painted by William Frye (1821–1872). A native of Austria, he was reared and educated in Vienna. He came to this country to paint the American Indian and arrived in Louisville, Kentucky, around 1845. Due to the strong competition in this area, he moved to Huntsville, Alabama, in 1847, and advertised his arrival in the *Southern Advocate* on March 5. This advertisement ran continuously for the year through June 10, 1848:

> William Frye Portrait Painter Has opened his Studio at the
> Bell Tavern; those who desire to have their portraits taken
> true to life, are requested to call and examine his
> specimens.

Frye found lodging with the William Hale family, and married their second daughter, Virginia Catherine. In 1854, George Wilhem Frye (William

Frye) took his oath of naturalization and became a United States citizen. He is buried in Huntsville.

Frye's competency as a painter is confirmed by his receipt of a commission from the Kentucky legislature to paint a full-length portrait of Henry Clay in 1865. The *Alabama Beacon* of Greensboro reported in 1868, "Gov. Bramlett [of Kentucky] in a letter to Mr. Frye . . . says: 'Your portrait of Henry Clay is a complete success and has my full approval.' The portrait, for which Mr. Frye received $3,000, is now suspended in the Senate Chamber over the speaker's desk."

Adrien Persac (1823–1873) was born in Lyon, France, and came to America around 1851. His rigid, symmetrical paintings (the ones of the plantation Shadows-on-the-Teche are excellent examples) reveal his primary occupation as a surveyor and civil engineer. Persac is listed in the New Orleans city directories from 1857 until his death.

Two of Persac's paintings of Shadows-on-the-Teche exist. One portrays the house from the bayou, the other shows the facade; the foreground figures in the latter view were actually cut from magazines and pasted onto the work itself.

William Henry Brown was one of the last silhouettists in this country. He was born in Charleston, South Carolina, in 1808, and was trained as an engineer in Philadelphia. His career spanned the period from the 1820s to the late 1850s, during which time he traveled from the Northeast to the Deep South. Mr. and Mrs. William Henry Vick met Brown in New Orleans in 1842, and invited him to their plantation, Nitta Yuma (which means "bear track"), in Vicksburg, Mississippi. While there, he executed five panels of pasties for the Vick's children. These pasties are examples of a design which introduces color and scenery to the silhouette, a rare nineteenth-century American art form. One of the panels depicts a lady (Mrs. Vick) on a horse, which a man (named Jake) is feeding. Close scrutiny shows that even the legs of the horse have been individually cut and assembled.

John Toole (1815–1860) was born in Dublin, Ireland, but after his father's death was sent to Charlottesville, Virginia, to live with his uncle, George Toole. John Toole was painting by the age of seventeen, and after his marriage he supported his growing family solely by his paintbrush. He traveled throughout the Piedmont and Tidewater areas of Virginia and possibly

Vue of the Huntsville Spring from Nature, William Frye.

Shadows-on-the-Teche, Adrien Persac.

Still life, found in Virginia.

Mrs. Sarah Pierce Vick on Horseback, William Henry Brown.

Skating Scene, John Toole.

Mount Vernon, George Ropes.

Central Kentucky Insane Asylum at Lakeland, Kentucky, Charles Edward Hughes, Jr.

Painting of the capitol, Montgomery, Alabama.

Montgomery True Blues at Camp Owen, **Alabama.**

74

South East View of Greenville, South Carolina, Joshua Tucker.

77

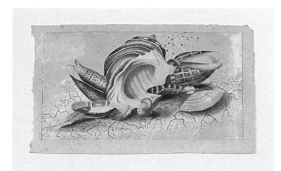

Theorem painting of seashells,
Emelia Smith Gernerick.

Zur Erinnerung, Louis Hoppe.

into North Carolina looking for work. Over three hundred documented paintings are known to exist, one of which is Toole's *Skating Scene*.

Ladies' folk paintings of the nineteenth century comprise a large body of work known as theorem paintings and mourning pictures. Painting in watercolor was part of the curriculum of the female seminaries and such "fancy work" was produced as memorials and decorative pieces for the home. The subject matter included portraits, landscapes, and religious, historical, and literary scenes. Most numerous, though, were memorials and fruit and flower still-life pieces executed on both paper and velvet.

Epidemics, such as cholera and yellow fever, were prevalent in the nineteenth century, and an estimated one out of every three children died. The mourning picture, either painted or embroidered, often provided an interior memorial for the beloved deceased. The format of such pictures included symbolic motifs such as the tomb, mourners at the grave, weeping willows, mourning doves, and trumpeting angels. Many examples were inspired by the large number of memorial pictures which appeared at the time of George Washington's death in 1799. The artists were frequently young girls memorializing family members and friends, although a number of mourning pictures have been found without inscriptions, which suggests that they had been prepared in advance for sale.

The work of a most talented artist is seen in the seashells theorem painting of Emelia Smith Gernerick (1754–1826) of Charleston, South Carolina. No stencils were used as they usually were in theorem paintings, but the Atlantic seashells were carefully drawn and shaded in a balanced composition. Of great interest is the veinlike seaweed growing from beneath the shells at the bottom of the drawing. At one time, it hung over the dining-room door of Strawberry Hill, the plantation that Mrs. Gernerick's only daughter and son-in-law built near Demopolis, Alabama.

Typical of the theorem still lifes is the work of Sarah Ferguson (1828–1900) of Jones County, Mississippi. One of her theorem paintings of flowers depicts large pink roses, rosebuds, and blue forget-me-nots flowering from a large basket. Close examination discloses the use of stencils for the roses and their leaves. Subtle shading with the watercolors shows an understanding and some knowledge of painting techniques.

Another aspect of folk painting comes in the form of calligraphy combined with watercolor pictures known as Fraktur. The word Fraktur was coined in this country in 1898 by Dr. Henry Mercer, first founder of the Mercer Museum in Bucks County, Pennsylvania. It refers to the fractured script used on medieval manuscripts. The script was used by the southwestern Germans in Alsace and Switzerland; some of these Germans immigrated to America and brought Fraktur with them when they settled in Pennsylvania. Originally Fraktur was an undecorated paper commemorating the birth of a child in script. A coin or token from the godparents was often wrapped inside the paper.

In America, Fraktur took many forms. Most common was the *taufschein* or birth and baptismal certificate. Hand-drawn Frakturs remained popular in America until the mid-nineteenth century when printed Frakturs became readily accessible.

Southern examples of Fraktur are found in Maryland, Virginia, and North and South Carolina. They represent the traditions of the Pennsylvania Germans who steadily migrated down the Shenandoah Valley in the 1730s to the mid-nineteenth century. Southern Frakturs vary only slightly in design from their Northern counterparts. The decorative elements are usually primitive, symbolic figures surrounded by a partially abstract border. Typical decoration includes hearts, angels, tulips, roses, and parrots which are painted in red, yellow, blue, green, and orange watercolors and outlined in black ink. Manufactured watercolors were available by the 1830s; otherwise, homemade colors were concocted by the artists according to old recipes. The ink was frequently made from oak galls, which contributed to the decay of the script areas of the piece.

The Fraktur artist was usually the local schoolmaster or minister who was able to read and write. The commissioned Frakturs supplemented their slender incomes. Due to their connection with Lutheran and Reformed parochial schools, these schoolmasters/artists were often moved from area to area. Upon their arrival in a new area, they would work off a backlog of accumulated birth and baptismal certificates and, of course, their work continued as new arrivals came into the community. Thus, unless specifically dated by the artist, the birth and baptismal dates do not reflect the actual date of a Fraktur's production. To expedite the work, the decorative parts of Frakturs were frequently completed in advance, leaving only the inscriptions to complete upon commission. These artists used both German and English cursive and block letter script.

Floral Cluster, Louis Hoppe.

Fraktur memorial, John William Leo(e?).

Vorschrift, Jacob Strickler.

80

Taufschein, Wild Turkey artist, Virginia.

Taufschein, Stony Creek artist.

A Bearthday Present, to LTK, Presented by Her Mother, Virginia.

Taufschein, unknown artist, Virginia.

Taufschein, Peter Bernhart.

Baptismal certificate, Peter Bernhart.

Confirmation certificate, Ambrose Henkel.

Ehre sey Gott in der Höh, Friede auf Erden,

Und den Menschen ein Wohlgefallen.

Jesus, wohn in meinem Haus, Weiche nimmermehr daraus;
Wohn mit deiner Gnad darinn, Weil ich sonst verlassen bin; O
du großer Segens-Mann, Komm mit deinem Segen an: Gieb, daß, Fried und
Freud, Glück und Heil, Diesem Hause wird zu Theil; Gleich wie Hiob und
Abraham, Reichen Segen überkam: Also schütte über mich, Deinen Segen mildig-
lich. Jesus, wohn in meinem Herzen, Wann ich leide Angst und Schmerzen,
Wann mich Armuth, Creutz und Noth, Drücket hat so helfet Gott; Wann ich
schon nicht Reichthum hab, So bleibt mir doch die Himmels-Gab; Muß ich hier
schon Armuth leiden, So bleibst du doch dort meine Freude.

Im Jahr Jesu Christi, 1740ten, — ten 15 ten Ist März

auf diese Welt geboren worden, von Christlichen Eltern, in Schillidalzsia Caunty,

Der Vater war Conrad Zolwig — Die Mutter war Elisobather eine geborne

House blessing printed by Ambrose Henkel, decorated by Peter Bernhart.

Jesus meine Freude

Hanna Elisabetha Clodfelder
ist geboren in Northcarolina, in Roe ... County, im Jahr
1807 den 28ten November ihre Eltern sind Johannes Clodfelder
und sein christliches Eheweib Maria Magdalena geb. Walk, sie
ist zur heiligen Taufe gebracht worden bey dem Herrn ...
luth. Prediger, ihre Tauffzeugen waren Hanna Walk
und Georg Frey. Jacob Crever was Born April 15th 1796

84

Reward of Merit, John Maphis.

Taufschein, Stony Creek artist.

Valentine, 1837.

85

Birth and baptismal certificate, Ehre Vater artist.

Scherenschnitte (cutout), North Carolina.

Scherenschnitte (cutout), North Carolina.

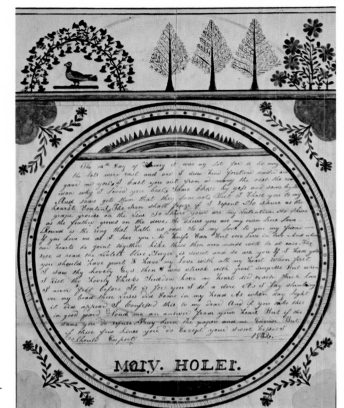

Valentine for Mary Holer, 1832.

Scherenschnitte (cutout), North Carolina.

A calligraphic form similar to Fraktur was the valentine, usually hand-drawn and scripted by untrained individuals and artists. The 1832 valentine for Mary Holer of Shenandoah County, Virginia, was probably made by her suitor, Reuben Bowers. Other such valentines were made by schoolgirls as part of their calligraphic and English exercises.

The early history of Fraktur artist Peter Bernhart's life has proven difficult to trace. He is known to have been in Keezletown, Virginia, as a post-rider from Winchester to Staunton beginning in 1789. Other records show Peter Bernhart as a cobbler and a schoolmaster, but his name is absent from the United States census lists of 1820 and 1830. Thus only his signed and dated Frakturs from 1789 to 1819, originating primarily from Rockingham County, Virginia, give substantial information as to his location. Bernhart had no training as an artist. Initially he peddled the prepared Fraktur forms by Friedrich Krebs of Dauphin County, Pennsylvania. His own work was colorful and symmetrical with a heart-shaped center shield for the inscription. His later works have printed inscriptions with appropriate blanks for

Taufschein, Joseph Kratzer.

Taufschein, Joseph Kratzer.

names and dates. He did, however, continue to decorate Frakturs by hand.

The anonymous "Stony Creek" artist was so named because more than half of his forty known works were for members of the Lutheran and Reformed Zion Congregation at Stony Creek in Shenandoah County, Virginia. A talented artist, he was both creative and masterful with his watercolor shading and design. Research by Klaus Wust has suggested that the artist was the teacher at Zion's parochial school on the Schwaben (Swover Creek)

87

"PR" Reg. Blutick's, trade sign
for bluetick hounds.

Flag and Banner Painting,
shop sign, Texas.

Valentine, North Carolina.

89

Taufschein, unknown artist, Virginia.

near Stony Creek. His works date from 1805 to 1824. The taufschein for Johannes Miller, born in Shenandoah County on August 8, 1812, displays his popular "heavenly curtain" design.

The "Ehre Vater" artist's work is known in Canada, Pennsylvania, and western North and South Carolina. The name refers to the artist's tendency to use a bold title such as *Ehre Vater und Mutter* (Honor Father and Mother). He is thought to have been an itinerant schoolmaster in the Lutheran or Reformed parochial schools. His work is well designed, colorful, and often geometrical. Some twenty-eight examples are known.

Jacob Strickler was born on November 24, 1770, in Shenandoah County, Virginia, in the Massanutten settlement where many Mennonites resided. It is thought that Strickler was either a Mennonite preacher or parochial schoolteacher. Strickler's ten known works date from 1787 to 1815, and include a Zierschrift, a secular writing example; two Geburtsscheine, or birth records; two Vorschriften, or writing exercises; three uncolored designs; and two major Fraktur drawings.

Study for Masonic apron, Sarah Ferguson.

Frontispiece, *Masonic Chart*, engraved by Amos Doolittle.

90

The Zierschrift is signed and dated: "1794, Jacob Strickler, residing in Shenandoah County, Virginia made this picture in 16th day of February." He comments further: "The paper is my field and the pen is my plow. That is why I am so clever. The ink is my seed with which I write my name Jacob Strickler." The upper section shows an exuberant array of colorful flowers growing from pots and hearts. These designs are frequently found in other examples of his work. The sawtooth design in the surrounding border and

Masonic apron, attributed to Alabama.

Bowl of Fruit, unknown artist, Virginia.

within the large initial "J" is another decorative element characteristic of his Frakturs.

It has been noted that Strickler based some of his design on motifs by Pennsylvania Fraktur artists, indicating a cultural communication between Virginia and the Pennsylvania Germans. More frequently, however, he copied his own work. Strickler's influence on the designs of Shenandoah County furniture decorator, Jacob Spitler, can be seen in a tall case clock (see essay on decorated furniture).

In the 1730s, the British introduced Freemasonry to America. Masonic aprons, both plain and decorated, were worn as a part of the fraternal regalia beginning in the late eighteenth century. Initially they were made of white lambskin, which symbolized innocence and purity. Later, however, silk or linen was used more frequently since both provided a better surface for printing or painting.

The decoration on Masonic aprons varies greatly. Some were never decorated, while others were decorated by artists commissioned by the lodge. Masonic iconography frequently includes a stonemason's tools; the all-seeing eye; the female figures of faith, hope, and charity; and the pavement, pillars, and steps representing Solomon's temple.

For the folk artist, Masonic aprons were an additional source of income. In 1803, Frederick Kemmelmeyer advertised in Alexandria, Virginia, that "he professes in the art of Free Masons Aprons on silk or leather and other implements belonging to the craft." Painted aprons were also produced by young ladies following stencils or copying engraved designs.

Stencilled aprons were frequently found in the South since the portability of the stencilling method was suitable to the itinerant artist. The designs on stencilled aprons seem to be based largely on an engraving of the "Master's Carpet" by Amos Dolittle in the 1819 book, *The Masonic Chart*.

Bryding Adams Henley
Birmingham Museum of Art

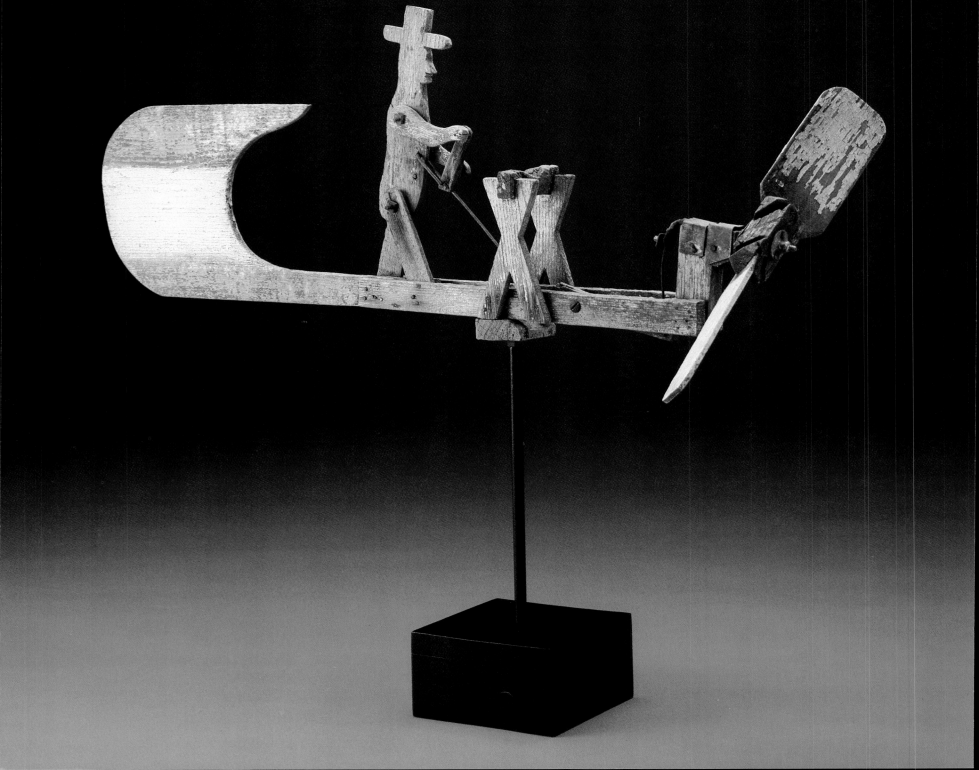

Sculpture

ike all artists, regardless of their background or era, early
Southern sculptors dealt with three primary factors in bring-
ing their work to being. The first, the three-dimensional nature of the universe, was the sculptor's playground; it separated
his work from paintings and drawings, which could only show
depth through illusion. The second, the need for materials, was
filled by the naive sculptor's use of local elements found in nature.
But it was the third factor, the artist's own imagination, which
courted creativity. Bound by tradition and eccentricity, it distin-
guished the naive sculptor from his "uptown" counterparts.
Therein lies the key to an appreciation of sculpture in the folk
culture of the South.

A vast array of three-dimensional objects from busts to birdhouses have been labeled as Southern folk art, but that description has been
interpreted in diverse ways by scholars and collectors. Concerned with tradition, folklorists have viewed pieces, such as gravestones, as reflections of not
only the stone carver's individual talent but also a shared community aesthetic. Others, however, have taken Southern folk art a step further to de-
scribe objects outside of the traditional motifs and the accepted settings for
artistic expression in the region. Such pieces are, in actuality, the end products of a single sculptor's eccentricities. Indeed, the terms *eccentric, naive,*

Policeman, found in Virginia.

95

Whirligig, Dr. W. J. Reynolds, Alabama.

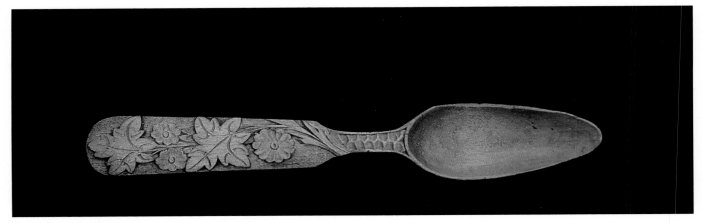

Carved spoon, Georgia.

and *primitive* have all been used in attempts to deal with works of untrained sculptors throughout the nation, but *folk* has become the layman's catchall for those objects. It is from that general definition that this overview of Southern sculpture grows.

Who was—and is—the naive sculptor in the South? The creative urge knows no boundaries; men and women, black and white, have made notable contributions to the sculpting tradition. Many European immigrants have added to the regional art as well. In most cases, objects were unsigned by their makers, and determining the provenance of specific pieces often proves to be impossible. Yet Southern sculpture favored by collectors today speaks of two types of three-dimensional artists and of divergent incentives behind their work.

One breed of Southern sculptor was the trade artist. In this class stood the figurehead carver, the signboard maker, the gravestone carver, and others. Normally trade sculptors were men. To these artisans, art was either their sole occupation or was an extension of their trade. As in the full-scale production pottery, sculptors may have worked in a factory-like setting. Others labored alone. The rural blacksmith, for instance, hammered out a host of mundane objects from plow points to hinges. The bulk of his products was strictly functional, and his talents were commonly hired out to

96

members of the community in need of a particular piece of ironwork. Certainly the average blacksmith was not following an artistic calling, but some went beyond the utilitarian demands of the objects they were making to embellish them with aesthetically pleasing twists and bends. Thus we find wrought-metal snake-eyed andirons, heart-shaped hinges, and twist-handled fireplace implements.

Today the trade sculptor has, for the most part, disappeared from Southern folk culture just as he has done elsewhere in the nation. His skills have been supplanted by the speed and standardized quality of industry, and the industrial designer, hardly a folk artist, is now responsible for the aesthetics of mass-produced articles. However, another breed of primitive artist, the home sculptor, remains active throughout the South, and it is likely that the incentives of these artists today have changed little from those of their earlier counterparts.

The home sculptor can be found in nearly every community, rural or urban. He or she is the self-taught animal carver living in a brick ranch house

Carved ivory fish and wooden box, W. A. Covart.

Poker, North Carolina.

Wrought-iron trivet, found in Virginia.

or the farm laborer whittling out a wooden chain in his spare time. Often such an artist has only pursued his talents in later years, particularly after retirement. But regardless of age, the home sculptor works, by and large, for his own amusement. Recognition and financial gain, though they may come later, are not the primary motivations behind his sculpting. As often as not, his pieces are not for sale to outsiders. They serve merely as decorations inside the house or as environmental pieces around the yard.

How true such a description applies to the pre-twentieth-century home sculptor is only conjecture, but there is no reason to doubt the presence of this class of artist in history. Of course, the neat categories of home sculptor and trade sculptor would strain under the complexities of the artists' lives if the details could be obtained. Yet the wealth of unsigned pieces ascribed only to a general region of the South will remain anonymous. Was this what the artist wanted? Was recognition unimportant? Or—more probably—was the average sculptor's world view such that he never imagined his pieces, or interest in his pieces, going beyond his immediate family and community?

The relationship between the Southern naive sculptor and his community cannot be ignored in viewing the artist's work as regional folk art. Unlike the quilter or the basket maker who often taught his hand skills to friends and family, the folk artist needed inherent talent which was refined through practice. Whittlers abounded, but few of them saw a face in the wood they were holding. Those who did had a different eye and a desire to create—two qualities that could not be passed on to the average individual. Thus sculpting is not traditional in the sense that abilities generally are not handed down from one generation to the next.

The traditional nature of Southern sculpture lies in the motifs and subjects which naive artists have favored for years. Lacking the progressive training which would have urged the sculptor to look for something entirely new, to break new ground, the unschooled sculptor was content with the themes he saw either in nature or in the work of other artisans. Hence it comes as no surprise that animals were a popular subject, and their images were sculpted in wood, clay, stone, and iron. This preference for common themes was the naive artist's tie to his community and folk culture, and it served to reinforce the cultural identity of both the artist and his audience.

Gun shop or hardware store trade sign.

99

However, some untrained sculptors did go beyond the typical subjects and choice of materials. The eccentric sculptor—a term which should not be taken in any negative sense—produced pieces which may seem bizarre or out of character when compared with the traditional, regional aesthetics, or equally significant, with the traditional role of art in his community.

As mentioned earlier, the Southern naive sculptor, like such artists everywhere, worked most frequently in media dictated by natural surroundings. Given the region's vast stands of timber, it is not surprising that the favored material was wood. In fact, there are few types of trees in the South that have not found their way into the hands of untrained artists. The rural artist in particular would have no problem finding abundant free materials even today. For some wood sculptors, a knife was a sufficient tool for the task, while the figurehead carvers of Baltimore surely favored more refined chisels.

Depending upon the artist, many wooden pieces were painted. Often this was to achieve a more realistic appearance, but many times the chosen colors surpassed the natural hues of the subject. The bright colors used on everything from architectural woodwork to toys have, through the years, taken on a pleasant richness. Indeed, some modern viewers might be shocked if they could see the original bold tones on works which have been subjected to decades of light and weather. The bright colors, however, were a welcome exception to the soft, sometimes monotonous tones of the natural woods which most often decorated the home and work environments.

Wood carvings have been found throughout the South in a variety of sizes and forms. Some of the largest were produced as trade signs for commercial enterprises. In most areas, the making of wooden trade signs was probably not a full-time occupation but rather one of the many duties performed by cabinetmakers or other multi-talented artisans. Trade-sign carvers worked in both relief and full three-dimensional styles, the relief style being predominantly a matter of lettering names and symbols on planed boards.

In creating more complex signs, the carver often sculpted a symmetrical object which appeared the same when viewed from opposite sides. Well-known symbols such as barber poles, oversized rifles, apothecary mortars, and the triple-orbed trademark of the pawnbroker were fairly standardized, but one-of-a-kind objects were also manufactured. In North Carolina, an

Trade sign, probably for a music shop.

Mortar and pestle shop sign, the Poydras Market, New Orleans.

immense, carved lyre marked the shop of a musical instrument maker. A mid-nineteenth-century jewelry store in Danville, Kentucky, promoted fashionable writing utensils with a carving of an eagle atop a mechanical pencil. Painted colors were a significant part of many of these commercial pieces, and the protection paint provided against the weather has surely been instrumental in the preservation of the surviving examples.

As a trade sculptor, the carver of signs lost his customers to the cheaper, more durable products of the twentieth century. One can only imagine the variety of this type of wooden sculpture that might have been seen in the nineteenth-century streets of large cities such as Charleston or New Orleans. It is interesting to note, however, that many of the traditional symbols and patterns of color—those of the barber pole for instance—remain in use today even though these signs are now mass-produced.

The greater urban centers of the South provided a market for certain specialized wood sculptors which was not available to the rural carver. In some ways, these markets were determined by the location of the city. This was the case for figurehead carvers, whose employment was keyed to boat-building centers on the coast. The cities of Annapolis, Baltimore, Norfolk, Charleston, New Orleans, and the District of Columbia were all known to have had working ship carvers. Many of these men produced a sizable number of pieces in their careers. As with several other trades of the era, figurehead-carving techniques were commonly passed on through lengthy apprenticeship programs, an acknowledged folk tradition.

For appearance and durability, figureheads were painted. Human forms and eagles were preferred themes. The magnificently sculpted figureheads were commissioned only for the finer vessels. The average working boat was not so artistically adorned. One exception was the wind-powered skipjack, a number of which are still in use in the Chesapeake Bay oyster industry. The skipjack featured relief-carved trail boards, and trail-board carvers remain active in the region even today.

The more typical, less specialized wood sculptors were not confined to specific localities, and general carvers have been documented in both urban and rural settings. The array of objects they created reflects a wide range of techniques, patterns, and imagination. Some were functional; others were more akin to novelties. Most were simply for display.

Preacher, attributed to Exell Greer.

Advertising sign for a jewelry store in Kentucky.

Overleaf: Model reputed to be of the State Department building, Washington, D.C., 1900.

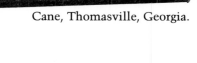

Cane, Thomasville, Georgia.

Cane, Virginia.

Cane, West Virginia.

106

One of the most popular works of the naive sculptor was the walking cane or staff. The cane was not only an art object but had a functional value as well, particularly for the elderly or lame. The cane was also a stylish addition to the male wardrobe in earlier times, but the typical primitive staff never saw the world of high fashion. Most canes were likely made for personal use or for use by a close acquaintance.

The basic materials for the walking cane were easily attained from the sculptor's natural surroundings. A long staff could be found in any grove of trees, but from that point, artists chose a score of different techniques and designs in transforming a stick into a piece of sculpture. The majority of Southern canes were carved in a relief style, and the artist worked basically with a flat surface wrapped around a cylindrical form. Limbs or slender trunks on which a twisting vine had imprinted a spiral easily became snake canes with the carving of a serpent's head near the handle. Even on smooth wood a snake climbing from tip to handle was a popular motif. Any number of animals from lizards to rabbits also found their way onto Southern relief-carved canes. Not surprisingly, alligators were a typical figure found on souvenir canes from Florida, but the alligator motif was not confined to that state alone.

Animals have not been the only subjects for relief cane sculpture. Political figures also held the interest of the Southern artist. A mid-nineteenth-century cane from Tennessee is decorated with the names of the states and the numbers of corresponding electoral votes carried by James K. Polk in the election of 1844. Another group of canes produced around the turn of this century and sold through a gift shop near Monticello celebrates the accomplishments of that area's most famous political figure, Thomas Jefferson. Relief inscriptions are combined with the images of a number of buildings connected with Jefferson. In many tourist areas, canes—and other sculpted objects—were made as souvenirs, and in such a setting, the carvings take on the guise of commercial art.

Various cane carvers chose not to embellish their creations with relief work but rather made complete use of the three-dimensional possibilities of the wooden staff. These artists transformed the handles of their canes into an imaginative variety of shapes. Again, animals were a popular design. The shaft of the cane was also incorporated as an integral part of the sculpture, sometimes as an arm for carved hands grasping assorted objects such as a fox horn or a snake. Remarkable combinations of full three-dimensional sculpting and low-relief styles appear in the work of many cane carvers. An early-twentieth-century walking stick (*left*) is adorned with a menagerie of creatures. Some are climbing the shaft, and others are bodiless heads protruding from it.

Also of note are ceremonial staffs associated with lodges and societies. An excellent example of this type of cane is the painted scepter attributed to a lodge in the Shenandoah Valley. The scepter matches a decorated box from the same hall, but the specific functions of the scepter and box are unclear. With a few exceptions, the extant Southern canes are one-of-a-kind objects, and even in the presence of occasional relief-carved initials or dates, the makers have usually remained anonymous. Apparently even the best of carvers rarely produced a large number of canes. Again, we can assume that

Cane, Georgia.

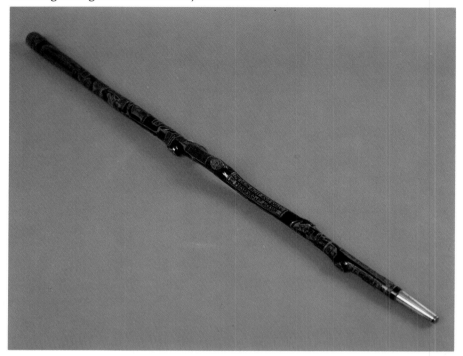

Walking cane given to President James K. Polk.

Man with a Snake, Edgar Alexander McKillop.

the typical cane carver was a home sculptor making walking sticks for himself and friends.

The larger body of Southern naive carvings stands alone artistically rather than as combinations of aesthetic designs and practical tools. These include a large number of wooden pieces embracing a broad range of themes. As might be expected, small animals of all varieties were sculpted, and most depicted the everyday pets, livestock, and wildlife associated with Southern living. Along the coastline, hunters used carved decoys to attract waterfowl. Other wooden birds served only as interior decorations. The carved eagle, a symbol of the nationalistic spirit, was popular as an architectural piece as well as a ship's figurehead.

Given the presence of serpents in folktales and legends, it is not surprising that snakes also appear in other objects besides canes as wooden sculpture in the folk culture of the South. The roughly crafted root snake, commonly decorated with paint, required only a minimum of carving and

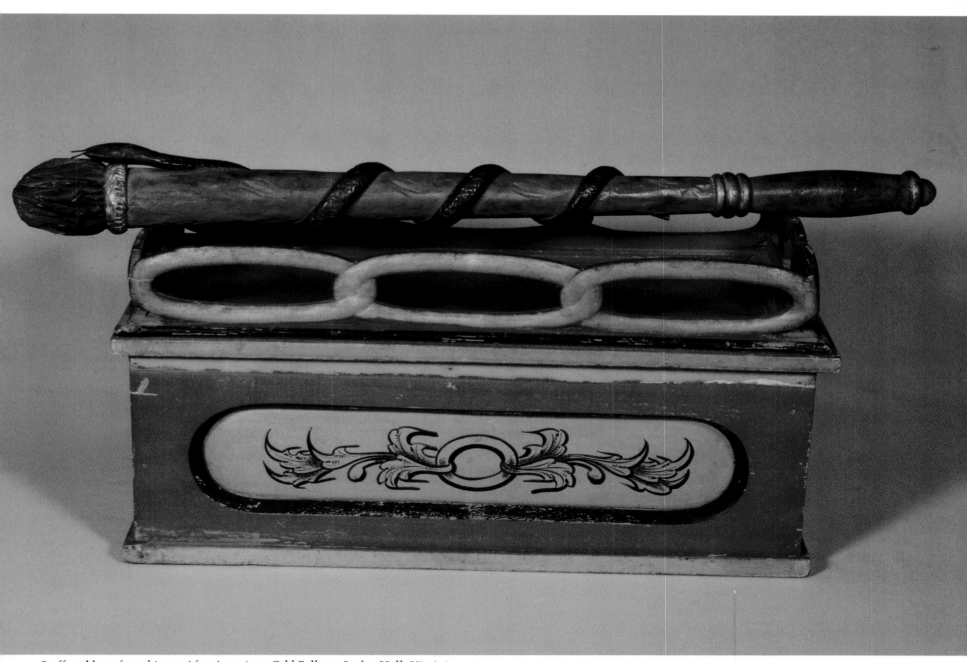

Staff and box, found in an Afro-American Odd Fellows Lodge Hall, Virginia.

Overleaf: Collection of North Carolina decoys and swans.

Owl decoy, Virginia.

Bear inkstand, attributed to Anthony W. Baecher.

was rarely realistic. On the other hand, jointed snakes, the carved pieces of which were held together with string or wire, could be made to writhe in the owner's hands. These were probably intended as toys rather than display objects.

The human form, too, has its place in the Southern sculpting tradition, and again the range of carving skills is quite remarkable. For children, there were wooden dolls of both races and sexes. These included one-piece toys as well as articulated creations with moving parts. An interesting example of the latter is the butter churner carved by W. A. Smith of Tacoma, Florida, in the 1880s. The hips and shoulders of this piece move when a crank is turned. Dolls were sculpted in clothed form or in the rough, to be dressed in hand-sewn outfits.

A number of carvings depict group scenes and activities rather than individuals. A few make comment on the human condition such as the *Wheel of Life* created by Pierre Joseph Landry in Louisiana in the 1830s. Landry portrayed the ages of man through nine stages which were all combined on a circular base. In a less meditative spirit, however, he produced a carving of himself spying on a woman bathing. The details of Landry's life are well documented and illustrate that the untrained Southern sculptor cannot be stereotyped as a coarse backwoodsman. Landry enjoyed a privileged life as a Louisiana plantation owner.

The human figure has been placed in more commercial or ceremonial settings in large carvings, but only a few full-figure wooden pieces are known to exist in the South. Some of these are carved Indians, the well-known symbol of the tobacco shop. Others honor famous individuals. In Lexington, Virginia, Captain Matthew S. Kahle, a cabinetmaker, sculpted a standing image of George Washington to crown the chapel of Washington and Lee University in 1840. Showing a good understanding of perception, Kahle distorted Washington's features so that they would look correct when viewed from below. Still other figures speak of the common man—a carved black figure in New Orleans served as a trade sign for slave auctions.

Throughout the South, realistic interpretations of worldly creatures—humans and animals—were certainly foremost in the sculptor's eye, but religious convictions carried over into art as well. For example, a simple

Top, first three decoys; second row, last three decoys:
Collection of factory-made and Louisiana decoys.

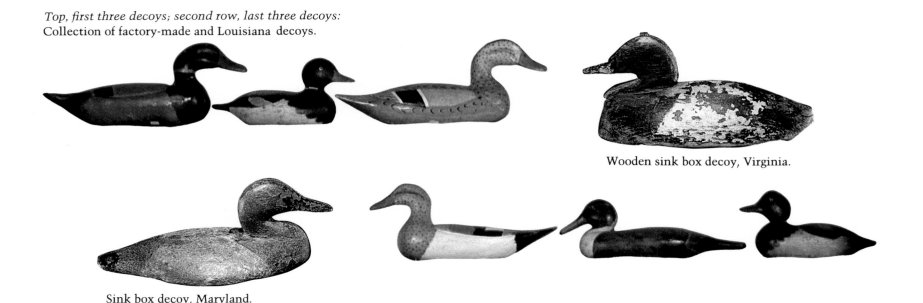

Wooden sink box decoy, Virginia.

Sink box decoy, Maryland.

late-nineteenth-century steeple ornament demonstrates the traditional symbol of the upward-pointing finger. In addition, Old Testament biblical stories have provided artistic inspiration for scene carvers.

Another group of wooden sculpture which was popular in the region might best be described as novelty carvings. Perhaps to pass idle time or possibly to exhibit dexterity with the knife, naive artists maintained a tradition of carving items such as wooden chains and balls in cages. These multi-pieced creations were crafted from single blocks of wood, and careful carving resulted in impressive flexible or movable sculpture. The novelty carving tradition continues to this day and is even embraced by chainsaw artists.

Not all Southern carvers limited themselves to what could be made from one wooden block. A few works illustrate a trend toward constructing sculpture from separately shaped pieces. In the late 1800s, Luther Goins, a Maryland carver, built an intricate wooden chandelier from hundreds of individual parts. Two decades earlier, A. C. Payne was constructing a model of the side-wheeler *Globe* in Tennessee. Such carvings are unusual, and the complexities of the final product often overshadow the skill invested in each small piece.

Painted wooden animals, Charles Pierce.

Group of cast-iron paperweights.

"Miss Chitty," North Carolina.

Doll, North Carolina.

Doll, North Carolina.

Doll, Jekyll Island, Georgia.

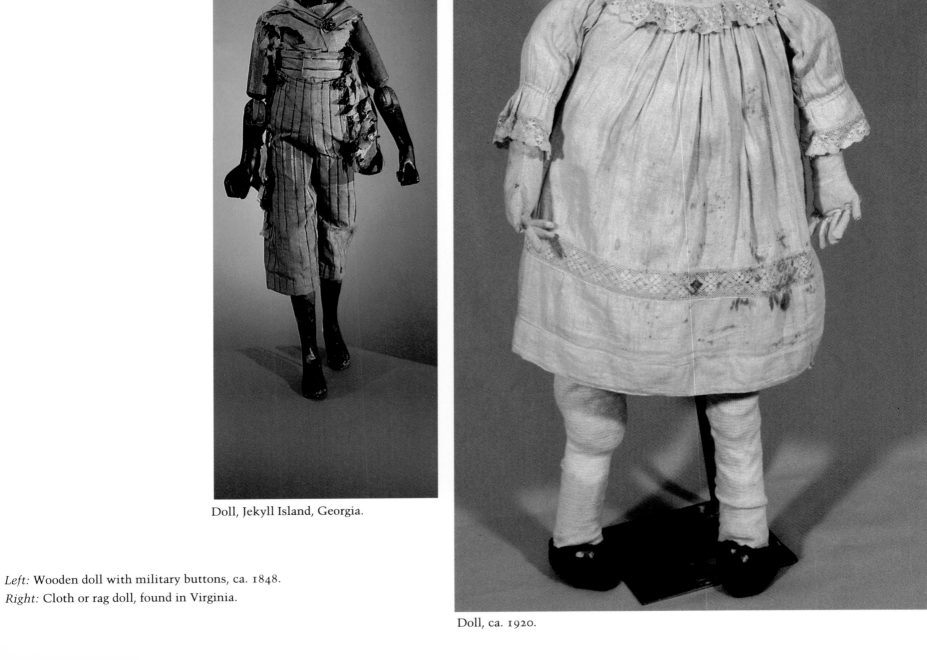

Left: Wooden doll with military buttons, ca. 1848.
Right: Cloth or rag doll, found in Virginia.

Doll, ca. 1920.

Toy doll churns butter when
crank is turned, Florida.

Doll, nineteenth century.

Doll, South Carolina.

Wheel of Life, Pierre Joseph Landry.

119

Self Portrait of Artist Observing Indian Maiden at Her Bath, Pierre Joseph Landry.

Carving by Edgar Alexander McKillop.

Close-up of statue of George Washington, Washington and Lee University, Virginia.

Statue of George Washington.

121

Church chandelier, Luther Goins.

Carved head, found in Tennessee.

Hand of God, steeple
ornament, Georgia.

122

Globe, steamboat model, Tennessee.

"Queen of Sheba" fiddle, Virginia.

Despite the dominant presence and workability of wood, a large number of Southern naive artists chose other materials for their sculpting. For instance, there were many stone carvers in the trade of gravestone production, though most of these might be more suitably labeled as craftsmen rather than artists. A few gravestones do, however, exhibit a great artistic bent. In North Carolina, pierced grave markers, which expand the typical low-relief technique of the traditional funerary slab, were set in cemeteries around Davidson County. Southwest Virginia stonemason Laurence Krone created a number of stylized headstones for his customers in the early nineteenth century, and full-sized human figures were sculpted for deceased Kentuckians in the Mayfield area. Nevertheless, most gravestone carvers just faithfully duplicated the established funerary forms and designs.

Outside of the gravestone tradition, there were few Southern artists who worked in stone. One artist, William Edmondson, a native of Nashville, Tennessee, produced simple limestone tombstones in the 1930s, but later refined his skills and carved animals, angels, biblical characters, human forms, flowerpots, and garden sculpture. At the time of his death in 1951, his work had been on display at the Museum of Modern Art in New York City and the Musée du Jeu de Paume in Paris.

Limestone appears to have been the dominant rock medium for stone carvers, but in the coalfields of the upland South, a few sculptors saw the black stone as more than just a source of fuel and jobs. One Bell County, Kentucky, miner carved a replica of the Bible in coal just prior to 1900. Contemporary coal carvings can now be found at Appalachian craft fairs.

More common than stone carvers were iron workers who decorated all varieties of utilitarian objects with artistic devices. Metal used as a medium for sculpture placed different demands on the artisan than either wood or stone. Two types of metal-working skills were common in Southern art: casting and wrought work. Though both resulted in a metallic, usually iron, object, each technique required totally distinct talents.

Casting involved the pouring of molten metal into a mold. The actual creative process rested more in the making of the prototype than in casting the duplicates. Prototypes could have been made in any suitable medium, particularly wood and clay. Most significant when viewing casting as sculpting is the possibility of producing literally hundreds of identical objects with

Tombstone, West Virginia.

Detail of grave marker in Mayfield, Kentucky.

Tree-of-life symbol on back of headstone, Virginia.

125

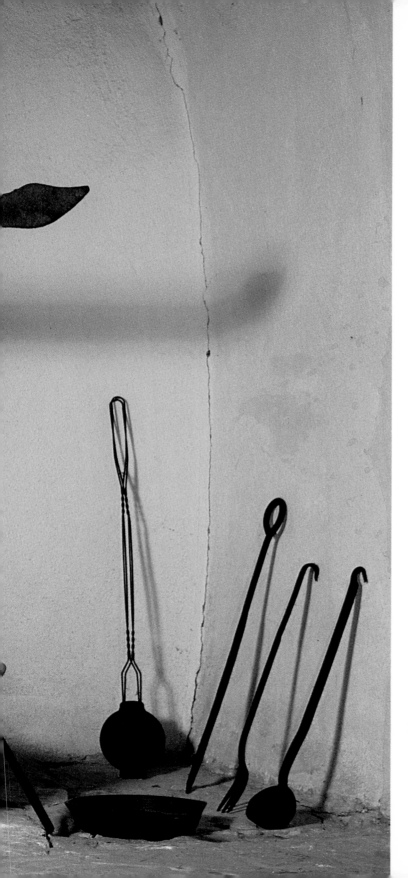

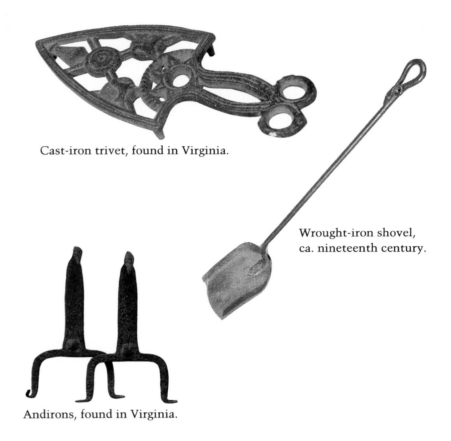

Cast-iron trivet, found in Virginia.

Wrought-iron shovel, ca. nineteenth century.

Andirons, found in Virginia.

Fireplace crane, Texas.

Wrought-iron graveyard crosses, Louisiana.

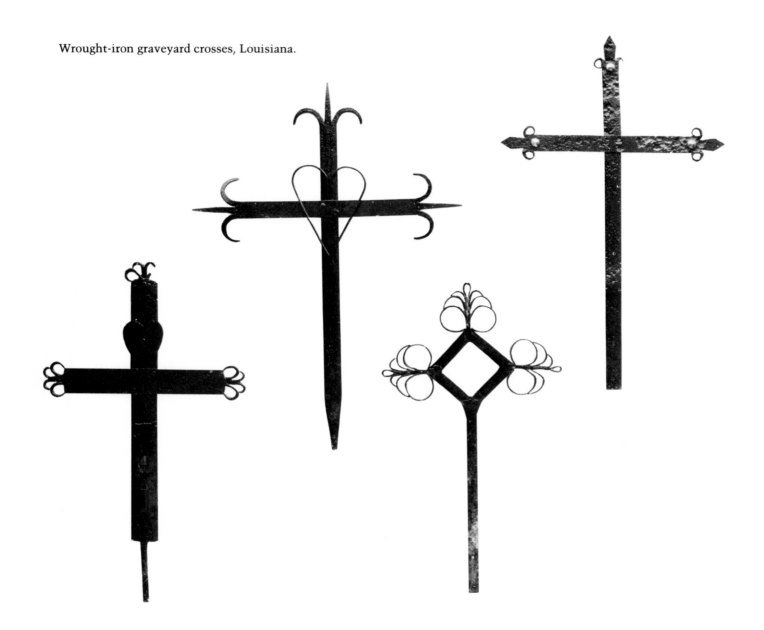

relative ease. The caster could mass-produce art, and indeed laborers not responsible for the original design could perform the actual casting.

Iron furnaces abounded, and the items molded in the industry reflected a score of purposes and designs. Of interest as sculpture are such objects as cast animals, andirons, stove plates, firebacks, and assorted household implements. The themes in cast sculpture were similar to those favored by artists who used wood as a medium. Human figures stood on andirons with their backs to the fire. The relief sculpting of stove plates portrayed scenes of man and nature. A cast parrot from Botetourt County, Virginia, could easily have served as a doorstop or a paperweight. With decoration, commonplace items attained increased aesthetic value.

A similar objective can be seen in the products of the many artistically inclined craftsmen who worked in wrought metal. The most visible of these sculptors were the blacksmiths. These men were essential to every community, rural or urban, but not all blacksmiths had the inclination or refined talent necessary to embellish day-to-day objects with artistic features. Judging the temperature of his metal by color, the blacksmith pounded, cut, and twisted iron into hinges, kitchen utensils, andirons, pokers, railings, gates, grave crosses, and even trade signs. Decorated examples of all of these have been documented in the South.

As a sculptor, the Southern blacksmith saw the same characteristics in an iron bar that the cane carver found in a wooden shaft. The snake motif thus appears frequently in wrought items as well. This motif is seen especially in long-handled objects such as pokers and fireplace shovels. On a more grand scale, wrought-metal artisans sculpted lacelike gates and ornamental ironwork in cities such as New Orleans and Charleston. Also in New Orleans, a unique wrought-metal trade sign hung on Bourbon Street as an advertisement for one smith's shop at the close of the nineteenth century. Even the simplest pieces exhibit a sensitivity not normally associated with the stereotypic blacksmith.

Key baskets, Virginia.

Double or courting dulcimer, found in Georgia.

Baptismal font stand, ca. 1875.

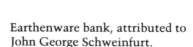

Earthenware bank, attributed to John George Schweinfurt.

A final class of metal sculptor in Southern folk culture chose sheet metal as a medium. Like the blacksmith, tinsmiths and coppersmiths primarily manufactured utilitarian objects, but their more artistic wares, particularly weather vanes, have long held the attention of folk art collectors. The wood-carver, too, produced weather vanes in the South, and both the carver and the sheet-metal artist commonly employed animal motifs. Some of these weather vanes are remarkable, full three-dimensional exceptions to the typical flat-relief style of sheet-metal sculpture. A compelling example of flat-relief work, a sheet-iron Indian, was crafted in North Carolina and originally rode under the headlight of a steam locomotive. Trade signs also proved to be suitable subjects for the sheet-metal artisan. Even in the construction of metal cupolas used to ventilate barns, craftsmen often exhibited impressive inventiveness in creating what can easily be viewed as three-dimensional art.

Of the naive sculptors in the South, only one group, the potters, had the

Stone carved in the shape of a
book, Mississippi.

*Chief Director of Mechanic Volunteer Fire
Company No. 1, Louisville*, Kentucky.

benefit of a soft, infinitely malleable material with which to work. Outside
of commonplace utilitarian utensils, these artists created an extensive body
of sculpture from face jugs to intricately constructed vessels. The Shenandoah Valley potters of Virginia were especially important in producing objects of the latter style. Few pieces anywhere can rival the child's bank
crafted by John George Schweinfurt in New Market, Virginia. However,
sculpting in clay was not limited to the upper Southern states. Nineteenth-
and twentieth-century ceramic grave markers still stand in Alabama, Georgia, North Carolina, Mississippi, Virginia, and West Virginia.

As can be seen, the Southern naive sculptor fashioned an astounding
assortment of pieces using a large variety of materials. Of special interest is
his diverse treatment of a limited selection of traditional themes. Few of
these artists, particularly those who worked outside of an established apprentice system, were likely to have received training. Therefore the learning process—and the tradition of sculpting—hinged upon observation and

Early photograph of the Aberdeen and Rockford Engine No. 35, showing use of a silhouette Indian.

Silhouette Indian locomotive ornament, found in North Carolina.

132

imitation. Beyond that, the naive sculptor relied upon personal creativity which sometimes bordered on the eccentric.

The role of three-dimensional art in pre-twentieth-century Southern folk culture was much the same as it was in other parts of the nation. While a host of functional objects were decorated with purely aesthetic features, many pieces had no practical purpose other than to be on display. The settings for such art ranges from doorsills to steepletops in both rural and urban environments. Seen today, the crude appearance of one work is offset by the refined quality of another, and if the present reflects the past, virtually no area of the South was devoid of untrained artists dabbling in three-dimensional forms.

Nevertheless, this cornucopia of motifs and techniques makes it difficult to approach Southern naive sculpture as a single body of work. Problems are compounded by the paucity of signed pieces and accurate histories. Still, the Southern sculpting tradition is too rich to be ignored or sloughed into a miscellaneous category. Appreciation for the handiwork of artists from the region continues to grow, and with it will come further questions, a perpetual shortage of answers, and the excitement of the discovery of new pieces.

Vaughan Webb
Blue Ridge Institute
Ferrum College

Decoys from Louisiana.

133

Decorated Furniture

The wide range of types of furniture in this chapter is a reflection of the many facets of the term *decorated furniture*. The diverse histories of the Southern states and the cultural groups that settled the different geographic regions explain this variety in styles and kinds of Southern decorated furniture. It is not possible to approach an overview of this furniture by states, regions, or schools; so it must be categorized by the types of decoration found on the furniture.

Southern decorated furniture takes many forms, styles, and shapes, from inlaid sugar chests to single- or multicolored painted storage boxes or blanket chests. However, the one aspect that is common to all of this furniture is that it comes from a strong craft tradition.

A craft tradition can be divided into three categories: home crafts, home industry, and community crafts. Home crafts are produced by people who have learned through necessity and are producing only for their own use. They may make baskets, preserve food, or perhaps make their own furniture, but they do not produce these crafts to sell them. Sometimes a person becomes very proficient at his home craft, which he probably learned through careful observation and, perhaps, imitation of others. His neighbors subsequently start to request his services, and he begins to sell his crafts to

Pie safe, Tennessee.

135

Safe with paint decorated tins, Tennessee.

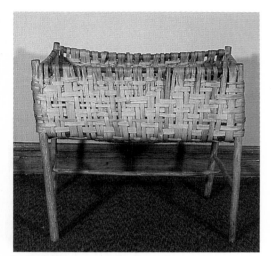

Baby basket or cradle, found in North Carolina.

supplement his main income, such as farming. Selling the crafts in this manner is known as a home industry. At the most sophisticated level of craft production are community crafts. In most cases these craftsmen earn a full-time living from their crafts and are true professionals who have apprenticed under a journeyman craftsman to learn the trade. The apprenticeship system was very strong in the South in the eighteenth and nineteenth centuries, having been brought to this country from Europe, and in most cases, it included a written contract drawn up by the courts for the parents and the journeyman craftsman. Most apprenticeships lasted from four to seven years, and during that time, the boy was taught a craft or trade in a formal teacher-student relationship. A study of these apprenticeship contracts reveals this was how many Southern furniture makers, or cabinetmakers as they are more correctly described, learned to make furniture. The quality of most Southern furniture also indicates that it was made by craftsmen who were quite skilled and certainly must have had formal training in the craft of furniture making.

There were many cultural influences on cabinetmaking in the South since there were several cultural groups that settled this area, namely, Germans, Scotch-Irish, Welsh, English, French, and Afro-Americans. There was also a vast migration of settlers throughout the South, with people moving from the North and settling for a while perhaps in Virginia or North Carolina, then moving on, maybe to Alabama or Texas, and, in many cases, later returning to an area where they had lived before. This resulted in much intermingling with other cultural groups and in an exchanging of ideas. Also it is important to remember that the frontier was moving farther west every day and was not isolated for long from the new ideas and influences coming from Europe and the North. By the late eighteenth century, items such as china and imported fabrics were available in what had only recently been the frontier, and throughout much of the South by the nineteenth century, if it could be brought in coastal towns, it could be bought anywhere that trade routes had reached. Particularly in the nineteenth century, backcountry Southerners were not isolated from information about the latest styles and trends. A great deal of correspondence was going on, newspapers were available, and people were very conscious of new developments.

This helps to explain that even though there are some examples of regionalism in Southern furniture and its decoration (such as paint decorated huntboards), there are few characteristics of style and decoration that label furniture as *Southern*. Since many of the same cultural groups that settled the South also settled the North, why should Southern furniture be very different? It is true that many Southern cabinetmakers used some materials that were not as abundant in the North, such as cedar, cypress, and poplar, and in some cases, this may help to identify a piece as Southern. However, the popularity of certain styles or decoration in different parts of the South usually had more to do with the cultural origins of the people than it did with the geographical area itself. For example, the appearance of the urn-and-tulip motif on blanket chests from Frederick County, Maryland; Wythe County, Virginia; Greene County, Tennessee; or Randolph County, North Carolina, stems from the culture of the people of German origin who settled there. This is a German rather than a Southern influence. While there are regional variations that show up in the South, there are few uniquely Southern traits. In general, any decorative styles found in the North will probably have counterparts in the South. This does not mean, however, that Southern cabinetmakers were unimaginative, for in many cases they created truly uniques pieces. One outstanding example is an inlaid slant-top desk found in Wythe County, Virginia.

Blanket chest with urn-and-tulip motif, Maryland.

Usually cabinetmakers made furniture to order, and since few of them had showrooms, a customer would often order "a cupboard like Mrs. Kegley's." References to orders such as these are often seen in cabinetmakers' account books, and so it is common to find a number of similar pieces within a small area. When more than a few similar pieces are found, it is often referred to as a *school* of cabinetmaking or decoration. The fact that customers would only buy what they liked and, usually, were familiar with meant that new cabinetmakers moving into a community quickly adapted their work to the preferences of the community. This was true both of the styles of furniture and of the decoration used on it.

Furniture was often decorated by different means; paint, carving, and some type of applied decoration were all common. Although recently many people have preferred the look of the natural wood grain itself, in the eighteenth and nineteenth centuries many homes had unpainted or whitewashed log- or wood-paneled interiors, and in such a room, undecorated

Inlaid slant-top desk of walnut and tulip.

Inlaid slant-top desk, open.

Dower chest with urn-and-tulip motif, Virginia.

furniture tended to look rather plain. Therefore, in order to make furniture more interesting, a number of decorative techniques were used.

Perhaps the most common technique was paint decoration; however, due to the more recent fashion of stripping furniture, relatively little Southern furniture has retained its original paint. It is obvious, though, from the amount of painted furniture still found in the South that this had been a popular means of decoration. It was an easy, quite inexpensive way to enhance a piece. It was also frequently used to disguise a less desirable wood, but hardwoods such as walnut, cherry, or mahogany were rarely painted due to their attractive natural appearance. It is interesting to note that occasionally furniture was painted to imitate pine and oak, though in many regions, pine was considered undesirable as furniture material and was usually painted.

Blanket chest painted green with panel bevels painted white, Eastern Shore of Virginia.

There are strong traditions of paint decoration in both the English and German cultures, and it is not uncommon in many of the other cultural groups that settled the South. The methods of paint decorating include a single color of paint, two or three colors of paint, paint graining, marbleizing, smoke graining, and painted decorative symbols and motifs.

The simplest, and perhaps most frequent, method of paint decorating was the use of a single color of paint. This had the desired effect of making a piece of furniture stand out from its surroundings, and, in many cases, may have enlivened a dark room. It is important to realize that over the last one or two hundred years, the paint will have oxidized and discolored or simply become coated with grime. Occasionally the paint was covered with a coat of shellac or varnish which will have darkened over the years and dulled the original color. Much of the paint used was very bright, even garish in color by modern standards, the common colors being red, blue, green, orange, and yellow. Probably the furniture painted this way most often were blanket chests or storage boxes. In Georgia, huntboards, or slabs, were often painted colors such as red, ocher, Spanish brown, and dark green.

Two or three colors were often used to further enhance pieces and particularly to emphasize important architectural details such as cornices and moldings. A first-rate example of this is a blanket chest from the Eastern Shore of Virginia which is painted green with the bevels of the panels painted white. This technique sets off the panels to advantage. Two other fine examples are flat wall cupboards, one from Virginia and the other from North Carolina. The cupboard from Virginia comes from Botetourt County and is painted orange with the drawer fronts, door frames, and part of the cornice painted dark blue. The one from North Carolina is painted red with the applied moldings, panel bevels, and drawer fronts painted black. There is also a slab from Georgia which is painted Spanish brown and accented with green decoration in the form of outlines, slashes, and stars.

Another totally different type of paint decoration which was done quite often in the South was paint graining. This involved painting a second color of paint over the original coat and, while the second coat was still wet, using combs or other utensils to remove some of the second coat of paint to produce a grained effect. This was often done on a piece of furniture made of an inexpensive wood, such as poplar or pine, to make the piece look as if it were

Orange-and-blue painted cupboard, Virginia.

Red-and-black painted cupboard, attributed to North Carolina.

144

Slab accented with green decoration, Georgia.

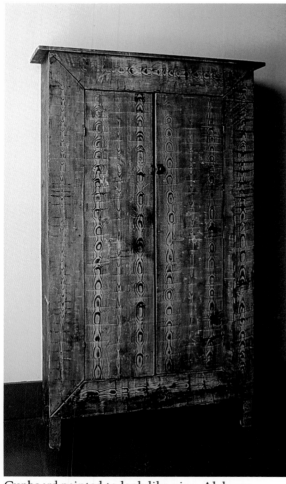
Cupboard painted to look like pine, Alabama.

constructed of a better wood, such as mahogany or walnut. However, in some cases furniture was grained to resemble oak or pine. Two excellent examples are a poplar cupboard from Alabama, which was grained to look like pine, and a chest of drawers from Kernersville, North Carolina, grained red and black to look like rosewood. Other techniques of applying paint include sponging and stippling. A good example of sponge decoration is a safe from Taylor County, Georgia, which has drawer fronts and lower door panels sponged with blue, green, and rust.

Two forms of paint graining that are fairly rare in the South are marbleizing and smoke graining. A storage chest with drawers that shows an overall gray-and-white marbleizing and a corner cupboard signed by Nathan Overton from Randolph County, North Carolina, with a marbleized cornice are good examples of the marbleizing technique. Smoke graining does not seem to have been a very popular form of decoration in the South, but examples have been found in the Shenandoah, Page, and Rockingham counties of Virginia. This effect is achieved by applying a base coat of paint and, while it is still sticky, blowing the smoke from a sooty flame onto the paint. After it is completely dry, a clear coat of varnish is put on the piece of furniture to protect the surface.

A very exciting type of decorated furniture found in the South is that with decorative symbols and motifs. This decoration is done freehand, with a template and compass, or with stencils. One of the most unusual examples of freehand decoration is a blanket chest from Piedmont, North Carolina, that stands on a high spiked leg with a unique scalloped skirt and has several different types of decoration: a tree in the center, ovals with dotted decoration, and fan patterns. A similar chest from Floyd County, Virginia, stands on a tall turned leg and has a star decoration in the center and what appear to be centipedes to the right and left of center. This, too, was done totally freehand and has dot decoration as does the North Carolina blanket chest.

A dower chest from western Maryland and owned by the Museum of Early Southern Decorative Arts exhibits a very unusual technique used to produce a different type of freehand decoration. In this case, a second color of paint was applied after the original coat of paint dried. A finger or blunt instrument was then used to remove some of the topcoat of paint while still

Chest of drawers painted to look like rosewood, W. D. Evans.

Sponge-decorated safe, Georgia.

Gray-and-white marbleized chest with drawers.

147

Corner cabinet with original paint and graining.

Washstand with smoke-grain paint decoration, Virginia.

148

Smoke-grained paint decorated box, Virginia.

149

Blanket chest with freehand decoration, North Carolina.

Chest decorated by Johannes Spitler, Virginia.

Blanket chest with freehand decoration, Virginia.

Safe with sailing ship tins.

wet to allow the base coat to show through and produce the pattern of decoration. Another example of freehand decoration is a birch bandbox from Bland County, Virginia, with flowers painted around the sides and an abstract floral design on the lid. A chest from Georgia displays freehand circles in red and mustard-colored hex sign motifs in the center.

Although decorated dower chests are seen more commonly in Pennsylvania than in the South, there are a number of outstanding Southern examples similar to the Pennsylvania chests. In this type of decoration, a template, and sometimes a compass, was used to outline the design which was then painted using several different colors of paint. The urn-and-tulip motif was commonly seen on the Pennsylvania chests. The Spitler chest, one of the most unusual in the country, also shows the use of a template and compass in the layout of the design. It is an outstanding example of geometric decoration.

Another fine example of geometric paint decoration is seen on a tall case clock from Shenandoah (now Page) County, Virginia. The paint decoration is attributed to Johannes Spitler and is one of only two case clocks known to date to have been decorated by Spitler.

The third type of decoration with painted symbols and motifs is stencilling, which is fairly unusual in the South. The finest of this *fancy furniture* made in America is from Baltimore. These chairs, settees, and tables with historical buildings, flowers, fruit, and landscapes as well as marbleizing and the paint-graining imitation of expensive woods are some of the most uniquely decorated pieces known. In all cases, there is a combination of stencilled as well as freehand decoration.

In sharp contrast to the sophistication of these pieces is the naiveté of the stencilled furniture from the school of New Market, Virginia. These decorated boxes of various sizes show the use of more traditional symbols and motifs and appear very primitive in comparison with the Baltimore pieces.

Applied decoration to furniture includes the application of punched or pierced designs on tin panels and the use of applied carvings on furniture. Occasionally the furniture itself was carved, but in most cases the carving was applied after the piece was made.

The use of applied punched-tin panels is seen more often on Southern

Tall case clock, paint decoration attributed to Johannes Spitler, 1800.

Sideboard with applied tin panels, Virginia.

152

Twig furniture, northern Appalachian or Shenandoah mountain region.

Pie safe with arch from the great seal of Georgia, ca. 1820.

Safe with applied tins, Virginia.

Mirror with walnut scroll-top frame, ca. 1800–1820.

154

furniture than on Northern furniture. Northern examples are usually limited to pie safes, pieces of kitchen furniture used for storing pies and cakes; applied tin panels on Southern furniture are found on corner cupboards, sideboards, architectural cupboards, and even flat wall cupboards as well as safes. Southern examples also make use of very interesting motifs including sailing ship tins on a safe from Alexandria, Virginia; the Georgia arch from that state's great seal on a Georgia safe from Greene County; and painted decorated tins on a safe from East Tennessee. An elaborate school of punched-tin decoration is found in Wythe County, Virginia, and employs a very stylized urn-and-tulip motif of German influence. The popularity of this type of decoration began in the mid-nineteenth century and continued into the twentieth century. Applied decorations may take several forms, such as applied carving, applied turnings, applied ironwork (decorative hinges, for example), and applied cutout decorations.

A flatwall cupboard from Franklin County, Virginia, illustrates the use of applied decorative hinges with terminals in a tulip motif, and the applied diamonds of a small serving table from Eastern Virginia were painted to contrast with the color of the piece itself. Both of these pieces present less common forms of applied decoration.

There is quite a lot of Southern carved furniture with the carving done directly on the piece itself rather than on an applied piece. Usually carved furniture is considered very sophisticated and formal, similar to the examples from Williamsburg, Virginia, or Charleston, South Carolina. However, there are a number of pieces that probably were done by cabinetmakers who were not trained as carvers, but were very good cabinetmakers. Perhaps a customer had requested that a piece be carved so the cabinetmaker attempted the work, resulting in a well-made piece of furniture with rather unsophisticated carving. The best example of this type of work may be a desk and bookcase from Piedmont, Virginia. This is a very sophisticated piece of furniture with a broken arch top and finely carved rosettes and shells, but the rampant hogs and the angel have a very naive or primitive quality to them. It is unusual to see such a combination of sophistication and naiveté on the same piece of furniture, but it may well be an example of a cabinetmaker experimenting with carving an unfamiliar subject. Three other pieces that show very naive but pleasing carving are a walnut scroll-top mirror found in Bull's Gap, Tennessee; a chair from Piedmont, Virginia,

Hunt table or server with applied painted diamonds, Virginia.

Chair with relief-carved snake, Virginia.

with a relief-carved snake on the back splat; and a bed from Kernersville, North Carolina, with an incised eagle on the headboard.

One outstanding example of original carving is the sofa from Texas carved by Christofer Friderich Carl Steinhagen, with very unusual fish carved along the top of the back of the sofa and with swan's head arm terminals. Perhaps the greatest piece of Southern carved furniture is a corner cupboard from Texas that was entered in the San Antonio International Exposition; it won first place, but the carver was so disappointed to win only a ribbon and no money that he gave the cupboard away. This cupboard shows applied carvings, relief carving on panels, and openwork carving.

Probably the most prolific and imaginative Southern decoration is the use of lighter colored wood inlaid on darker woods to create decoration on furniture. It is one style of decoration that is found in virtually all parts of the South. The use of inlay probably began about 1800 and continued through 1900. Inlaid decoration is made with many types of wood and is found on many styles of furniture including Chippendale, Hepplewhite, Sheraton, and Empire. Inlaid furniture is usually made from dark wood, such as mahogany, walnut, or cherry, and inlaid with any light-colored wood, such as dogwood, holly, or maple.

The patterns inlaid on Southern furniture are extremely diverse and often very imaginative. There are definite schools of inlaid furniture and there are also some common themes which appear in many states in slightly different forms. One example of a theme seen many times is the running-vine inlay, variations of which can be seen on different pieces of furniture from clocks to blanket chests, chests of drawers, and armoires.

Blanket chests are among the most common form of furniture decorated with inlay in the South. One good example from the Shenandoah Valley of Virginia has names, dates, and places as well as heart motifs carved on the chest. From South Carolina is a walnut bracket-foot blanket chest with an inlaid border and a central motif of an urn with a variation of the running-vine motif. There is a small walnut blanket chest from Georgia with panelled ends and front, maple and cherry inlay of a star and stylized trees, and other undefinable motifs.

Bed with incised eagle on the headboard, North Carolina.

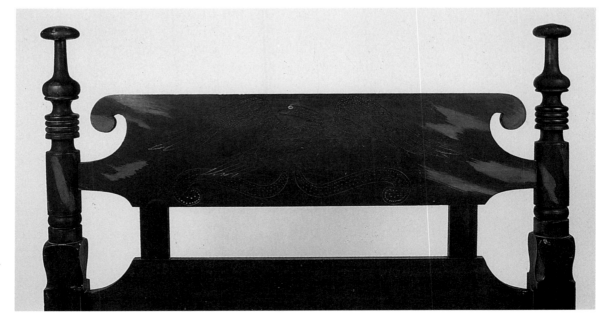

Close-up of headboard with incised eagle.

Sofa by Christofer Friderich Carl Steinhagen, Texas.

Desk and bookcase with walnut and light wood inlay, Kentucky.

Corner cupboard with applied, relief, and openwork carving, Texas.

Walnut chest with maple and cherry inlay, Georgia.

Corner cupboard with inlaid birds and rope and tassels.

160

Small chest with inlaid house, East Tennessee.

Table with inlay of bellflower-type motif, attributed to Tennessee.

Painted and inscribed chest, North Carolina.

Huntboard with red-and-black sponge decoration, South Carolina.

Chest with inlaid names and hearts, Virginia.

An unusual piece from East Tennessee is a small chest (possibly a sugar chest) with an inlaid house with a chimney. Also from Tennessee is a very unusual school of inlay consisting of a number of corner cupboards which have hens or roosters inlaid on the lower doors, certainly an interesting motif. These cupboards also show the rope-and-tassel inlay peculiar to this part of East Tennessee and seen on many other pieces from this area which do not have the chicken motif.

One of the most pleasing pieces with inlay is a desk and bookcase from Danville, Kentucky, that is walnut with both walnut and light wood inlay designs that include the common urn and running vine, barber's pole, fans, and stars.

Two of the most eccentric pieces of inlaid furniture from the South are tall case clocks. A clock from the central Piedmont of North Carolina is walnut with light wood inlays representing vines, hearts, eyes, a mouth, tulips, stars, a fylfot, a moon, fans, and lunettes. The clock from Pulaski County, Virginia, made by Peter Rife in 1809 is cherry with veneers and orange, green, and natural wood inlay representing urns, vines, tulips, flowering plants, stars, eagles, drapery, and several borders of alternating patterns. It also has carved rosettes in the broken arch top and a turned central finial with hand-carved finials on the right and left sides of the bonnet. It can be seen, therefore, that Southern inlaid furniture includes everything from very simple neoclassic-line inlay and diamond keyhole escutcheons to very imaginative and detailed decorative motifs.

Decorated furniture comes not only from the backcountry but also the urban centers of the day; we find Southern decorated furniture in all styles, periods, and forms. Whether reflecting cultural identity, religious beliefs, environmental influences, or simply current fads, Southern cabinetmakers made good use of popular decorating techniques.

J. Roderick Moore
Blue Ridge Institute
Ferrum College

Case clock with light wood inlay.

Painted chest with cutout heart in apron, Virginia.

Textiles

stable society had developed along the Chesapeake by the late seventeenth and early eighteenth centuries. A network of towns was evolving, including Annapolis, Yorktown, Edenton, Williamsburg, Norfolk, and Charleston. Small urban and cultural centers were developing along the Tidewater and lowland areas of Maryland, Virginia, and the Carolinas. Although some homes were quite elegant, others were furnished with only the most essential objects. Textiles were always among the most necessary and costly items in any household.

The 1690 inventory of the Virginia estate of Robert Ruffin illustrates the monetary dominance of textiles in the household. The value of his table and eighteen leather chairs was equivalent to 700 pounds of tobacco. Four heifers were valued at 1200 pounds, while one feather bed, bolster, two pillows, bedstead curtains and valance, a bed rug, and a blanket were valued at 1400 pounds. Another Virginia inventory of 1693 listed three pounds of woolen fringe for valances valued at eleven shillings compared to a silver-headed cane and gold ring at ten shillings (Poesch 1983, 28). One nineteenth-century gentleman was so distressed at the loss of a leather trunk containing four quilts that he ran a

Detail of Crazy Quilt (*page 166*).

167

Crazy Quilt, Georgia.

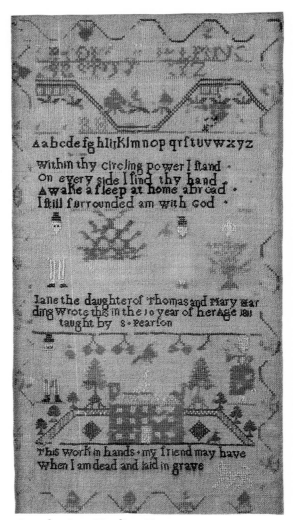

Sampler, Jane Harding, Tennessee.

View of Saint Joseph's Academy near Emmitsburg, Maryland, Henrietta Virginia Wheeler.

169

notice in a Savannah newspaper with a detailed description of his bedcoverings, offering a reward for information or their return. The high monetary value placed on textiles clearly indicates their importance.

Southern textile styles varied little from those found in the North. Settlers in both areas relied on European models for style, form, and technique, adapting them as necessary. Samplers, quilts, coverlets, homespun fabrics, and bed rugs were found in both the North and South. Southerners, however, proved to be more successful in silk making than their Northern counterparts and produced substantial quantities. Velvet, silk, fine linen, and calico were used more frequently in the South than in the North, especially during the eighteenth century when the South was closely bonded to England whose goods were more readily available and more stylish than those of New England. This use of fabric is especially apparent in the early quilts. Southern quilts were made with more elegant fabrics and possibly finer stitching than those in the North.

Many areas of the South remained rural and dependent upon home-manufactured goods longer than the more urbanized North. Thus some traditions and techniques of textile production existed longer in the South. However, due to the migration of people, purely regional textiles were rare. One exception was the products of the Louisiana Acadians, whose regional isolation fostered a distinct textile tradition and showed the richness and diversity inherent in traditional procedures.

Though many fabrics were imported from England in the eighteenth century, a large portion were created by American women. Every woman was taught to sew, and many were responsible for doing, or at least supervising, all of the plain sewing for the household including clothing, bedclothes, and towels. Producing the clothing essentials for a household, which often included not only family members but slaves, was an enormous task. Yet women still found time to create the special objects of beauty that we collect and admire today: the finely woven coverlet, intricate embroidery, or flamboyant quilt. Needlework provided one of the few outlets for women to express their artistic talents. Creating a bedcover, for example, offered an opportunity to shape the interior environment; it gave women options—the chance to make the choice of a pattern, fabric, and color. Occasions such as quilting bees also offered social interaction with other women, a rare treat for many women isolated on a farm or plantation.

In the eighteenth century, there were three distinct categories of needlework: plain sewing, marking, and fancywork (Swan 1976, 9). Plain sewing consisted of such basics as hemming, seaming, and making everyday clothing. In order to identify the household fabrics, each item was often marked with cross-stitched initials, numbers, or dates. Knowledge of these basic skills was necessary for almost every woman. Fancywork, on the other hand, was usually executed by the more well-to-do young girls whose parents could afford to send them to school or provide them with special lessons.

A young girl's first needlework project was a sampler. With their variety, intricate stitches, and often humorous or sentimental verses, samplers ranked among America's most outstanding textile achievements. They were originally intended to serve as reference books of stitches and designs, or as examples of the needlewomen's skills. Linen was the most common ground fabric, although wool and cotton were used occasionally. Some nineteenth-century samplers were executed on canvas. Embroidery threads were usually silk or linen, but by 1830, Berlin wool yarns also became popular as sampler threads. Painting later replaced some of the more time-consuming needlework on embroidered pictures.

Sampler, Eliza Parry, Georgia.

Samplers of the late seventeenth and early eighteenth centuries were typically long and narrow. As these early samplers served primarily as a record of patterns and stitches, they were rolled away when not needed for reference. Young girls between the ages of five and twelve began making samplers to learn how to work letters and numbers, skills which could then be transferred to the marking of household linens. Later in the century, girls began to add pictorial designs to their work, and there was a shift from basic recording to making a decorative object. Samplers took a more square shape, usually having a border. They became elegant and elaborate examples of a young girl's needlework, often framed and displayed in the home.

Girls' schools and academies were prevalent in the late eighteenth century and many samplers are the products of the training in those institutions. Most schools offered a variety of subjects, but reading, writing, geography, languages, study of the scriptures, and the rudiments of arithmetic (to aid in household accounts) were emphasized. In addition, most schools offered instruction in music, dancing, drawing, and needlework.

Southern states have not yielded the scores of samplers found in the North. There is the possibility that not as many were made in the South, but

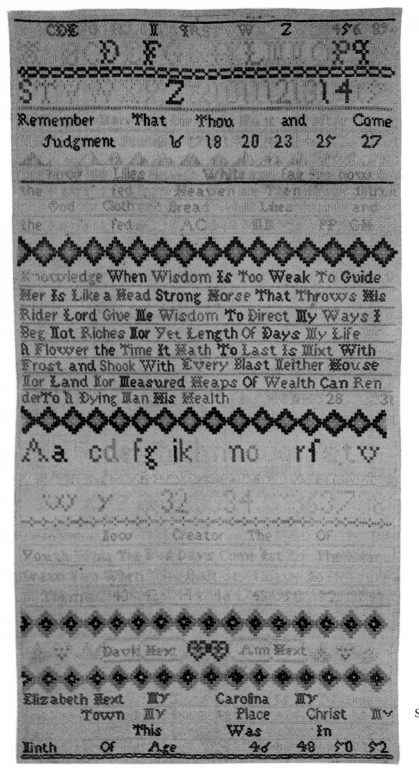

Sampler, Susannah S. Rees(e), Virginia.

Sampler, Elizabeth Hext.

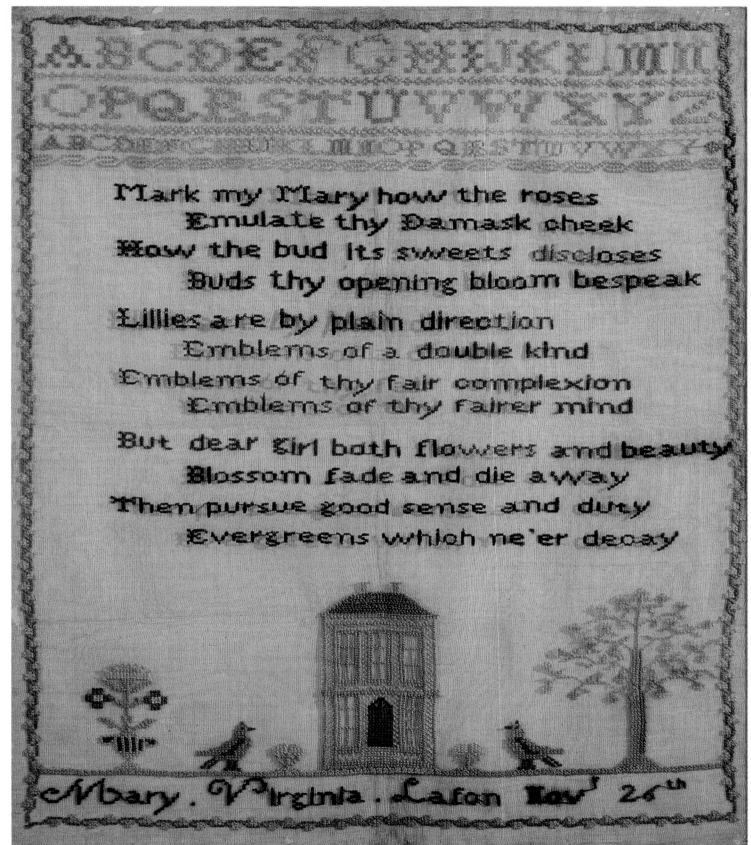

Sampler, Mary Virginia
Lafon, Kentucky.

Sampler, Caroline Broughton
Fabian, Georgia.

Sampler, Sarah Ann Randall.

174

Sampler, Harriet W. Higgs, North Carolina.

Sampler, Mary Harrison, Virginia.

Sampler, Alcinda C. Timberlake, West Virginia.

Sampler, Mary Lou Hawkes, North Carolina.

Mourning embroidery, Susan Creamer, Maryland.

Sampler/picture, Jane Winter Price, Maryland.

this seems unlikely with the number of female academies and instructors offering private instruction. There is still much research and fieldwork to be done in this region, and as this is accomplished, more objects, including samplers, will probably come to light.

In addition to samplers, other popular needlework items included canvas work (needlepoint), crewelwork embroidery, cutwork, and drawnwork. Crewel yarns and fine canvas work were used to produce some of the most elegant and engaging chair seats, pocketbooks, and pictures of the eighteenth century. Instruction was offered in technique and in drawing one's own design on canvas. Imported canvas, which often carried pre-drawn designs, was very expensive. Designs were rarely original; students frequently copied models presented by their teachers. Popular prints were often the source of many pictorial designs. *The Sacrifice of Isaac* (the earliest known Southern embroidery of its kind) worked by Elizabeth Boush in 1768/1769, was probably copied from an engraving published in Antwerp in 1585 by Gerard de Jode. De Jode's volume was a popular source for needlework designs. Illustrations from sixteenth-century Bibles influenced the design of biblical embroideries throughout the seventeenth and eighteenth centuries. The compositions were preserved over the years; in fact, Elizabeth Boush may never have seen the original de Jode print but only other embroidered pictures derived from it (Ring 1977, 3:1–19). In cutwork, only the edges of the design were embroidered. The intervening background fabric was then cut away. Various embroidery stitches refilled the open areas. Drawnwork was an openwork design where threads were pulled aside and gathered in clusters, leaving openwork patterns. In some cases, threads were carefully withdrawn from the pattern area while the remaining threads were worked together to form the design. This type of work was to be found on samplers, table covers, and bedcovers, often in conjunction with elaborate all-white embroidery, and was widely popular in the South.

In making bedcovers for their households, women not only produced utilitarian textiles which would afford warmth, but also created outstanding examples of needlework with a brilliant sense of color and design. Bedcovers included the coverlet, bed rug, and quilt—the most popular bedcover.

Sampler, Louisa Nenninger, Maryland.

Pieced snake quilt, North Carolina.

Quilts were composed of three distinct layers—top, interlining, and backing—which were all wrought with a needle. The top of the quilt was made first and could take one of three forms. It could be what appeared to be a single piece of fabric, but was actually two or three lengths seamed together. The top could also be constructed by sewing small bits of fabric together to form an overall pattern. Appliqué, the third technique, involved sewing pieces of fabric onto a larger, background cloth. The cutout pieces, when arranged on the ground fabric, formed the overall design. All three techniques continue to be popular in modern quilting.

Several different substances could be used for quilt interlinings, though wool and cotton were the most common. Cotton, for obvious reasons, was used almost exclusively in the South. When necessary, other batting alternatives could include cast-off clothing, paper, rags, or even another worn quilt. Ideally, an interlining was soft, warm, and easily sewn through.

Backing fabrics varied considerably. Sometimes a new piece of cloth was purchased, but more often the backing was a combination of fabrics salvaged from another source. Flour and sugar sacks were popular backing materials in the nineteenth century, often still displaying a faded stamp.

The top, interlining, and backing were fastened together by small, regular stitches worked in orderly patterns known as quilting. The simplest design followed the piece, outlining the shapes of the top pattern. A more elaborate quilt would have had ornamental designs worked into the empty spaces and the other areas quilted with a series of lines, shells, diamonds, or other shapes. If the quilting followed the piece, no special marking of the top was necessary. However, ornamental work required that the pattern be marked on the surface before quilting began. The design was traced with a pencil or chalk around the desired pattern. When the top was marked and ready, the three layers were basted together and placed on a quilting frame that held the layers tightly to insure even stitches. Quilting could be the work of a single person or a social gathering, such as the quilting bee. Cotton tape or a separate strip of fabric was used to bind the quilt edge, although the backing fabric was sometimes brought over the edge and sewn down.

Patterns for tops and quilting designs were traded among friends and published in newspapers and ladies' magazines. This, coupled with the constant migration of people, makes regional distinctions difficult, if not impossible, to detect. State and county fairs, popular in the nineteenth century,

Baltimore Album Quilt, Maryland.

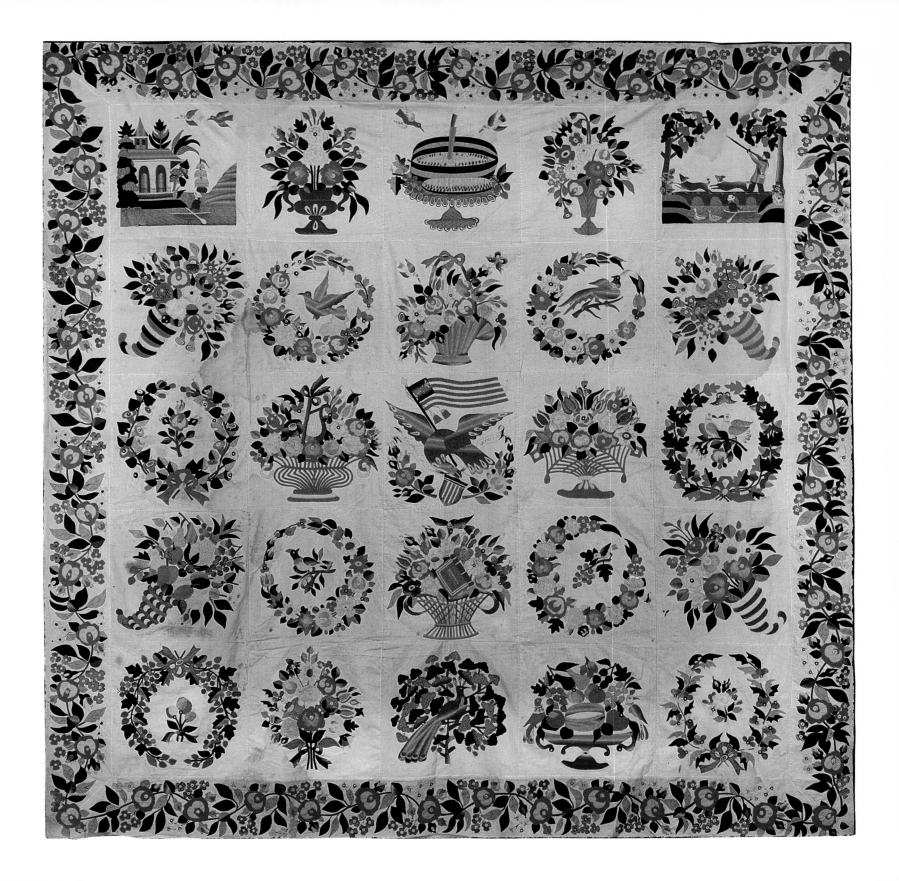

Unquilted spread of cotton and chintz, Maria Boyd Schulz, South Carolina.

were another source for patterns. Quilt making, along with other homecrafts, was encouraged by the annual county fairs. Prizes were usually awarded for the best work in each category. Fairs for philanthropy were also very widespread in the South, as Virginia Gearhart Gary describes: "About 1840 an epidemic of fairs broke out among the Southern women whose activities were later rivaled by famous benefits in the Northern cities during the Civil War. Ladies industriously plied their needles to provide many articles for the fair" (Gary 1928, 2:264–79). The benefits from the fairs were usually for the church, orphans, or, occasionally, for the preservation of a historic house. Patrons paid to view the fancy needlework which fostered the exchange of patterns and techniques.

One of the most well-known examples generated by a philanthropic benefit was the Alabama *Gunboat Quilt* made by Panthed Coleman Bulluck of Greene County, Alabama, before October 19, 1860. Her descendant, Mrs. Hatter of Greensboro, Alabama, whose two sons were in the Confederate service, donated this quilt to the war effort to raise money to buy a gunboat for the South. Mrs. Hatter's minister, the Reverend J. J. Hutchison, raffled this quilt not once but over and over again. By agreement, each winner would donate the quilt again for the Confederate cause, thus its name.

Because of climate and availability of raw materials, cotton was the most commonly used fabric in Southern-made quilts. Beyond that, there are few common elements. Quilts were, and are, the personal creations of their makers. Influenced by traditional patterns and availability of materials, each still bears the mark of its creator, canceling the possibility of strong and identifiable regional characteristics and distinctions.

Because economic and physical conditions in the colonies were difficult, early quilts were rudimentary, constructed of available fabric in simple designs with only enough quilting to bind the layers. As conditions improved, so did quilt design. By the middle of the eighteenth century, the colonies reached a stable, relatively affluent level, with a population of almost 1,500,000. For the quilter, there was a greater amount and variety of domestic and imported fabrics which offered a broader range for creative expression. Indian chintz, printed with exotic floral designs, was the vogue in Europe and was available along with bright calicoes and silks. A quilter

Quilt made on the William Alston plantation, South Carolina.

Floral Album Quilt, Georgia.

Framed-center style quilt, Martha Hobbs Lucas, Alabama.

was finally able to design and execute a predetermined pattern with a wealth of fabrics for her selection.

A popular quilt design during the last quarter of the eighteenth century was the framed-center style. The designs, especially bird and floral motifs, were usually cut from English (later American) chintz and appliquéd onto a cotton ground. Appliquéd bedcovers were very popular in England and America, and soon textile printers, notably John Hewson of Philadelphia, were designing patterns specifically for quilts and for the sale of imprinted squares. The designs combined bold motifs to be used as the center; wide and narrow strips of flowers, leaves, or birds to form borders; and smaller sprigs of flowers or groups of animals to be used as accents or ornaments. It is in appliqué that we see the quilter's artistry given full rein. The imaginative pictorial elements of the bedcoverings indicated the fine sense of design possessed by many of these talented quilt makers. For example, the maker of a Staunton, Virginia, marriage quilt used depictions of the bride and groom (he with military epaulets) as the central square and surrounded the couple with a multitude of flowers, leaves, and birds. A few Masonic symbols also appeared in one of the blocks. An Arkansas quilt, bordered by a meandering floral vine and pots of flowers, illustrates Adam and Eve's flight from the Garden of Eden.

Highly decorative and intricately worked chintz quilts reached their zenith of popularity from about 1820 to 1840. This style was especially popular in the South, and many outstanding examples were made in the region, notably the quilt produced on the William Alston plantation near Charleston, South Carolina, about 1830. A detail of the "Hunt Cornucopia" is the center square motif. Two other complete squares have been cut in half diagonally and set against the sides of the central square. Between two dark borders is a white border with a strip of branches holding appliquéd birds and butterflies. The three remaining borders are actually one piece of printed chintz.

A prevalent quilt style in the mid-nineteenth century was the Album Quilt. These quilts were usually a cooperative effort intended as a gift for an honored recipient such as a bride, minister, or teacher. Because the quilt blocks were individually made, each participant was able to exercise some independence in their choice of color and design. The blocks were usually

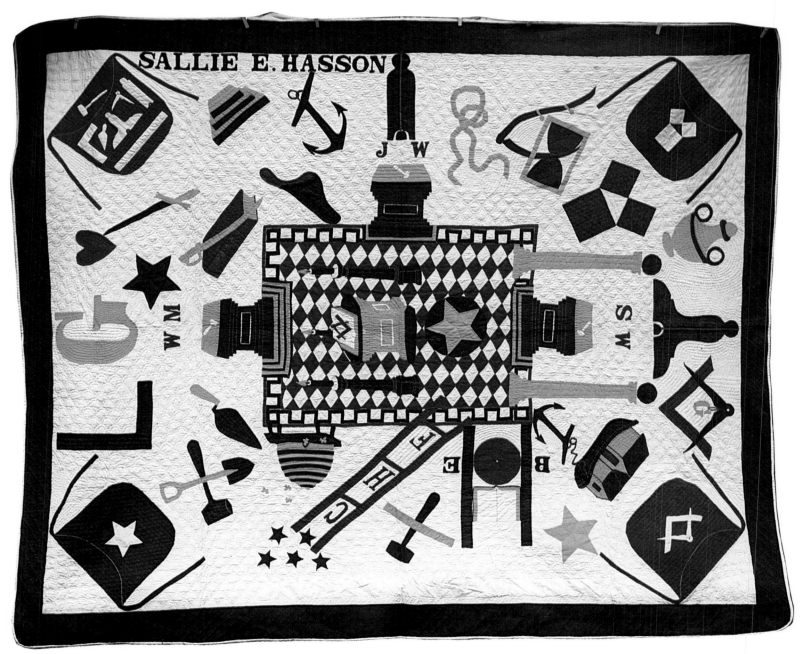

Masonic quilt, Sallie E. Hasson, East Tennessee.

Adam and Eve in the Garden of Eden and Their Flight, ca. 1900.

Baltimore Album Quilt, Maryland.

Album Quilt, probably Baltimore.

Album Quilt, ladies of Greene and Hale counties, Alabama.

pictorial and appliquéd, though pieced, geometric Album Quilts were also made. Blocks were inscribed with the donor's name and date, creating a useful historical record.

A distinctive group of Album Quilts was made (the finest between 1846 and 1852) in Baltimore by a company of young women who called themselves the Ladies of Baltimore. These skillful needlewomen worked together to make quilts, known as Baltimore Album Quilts, for friends, clergy, and for sale for the benefit of the church. They may have been inspired by an older woman, Achsah Goodwin Wilkins, who was an expert at creating highly original, decorative arrangements with fabric (Katzenburg 1981, 64). Wilkins's examples encouraged a departure from traditional piecing to a more complex design utilizing a greater range of fabrics, more proficient needlework, and sophisticated appliqué techniques. The workmanship of many of the Baltimore Album Quilts was so distinctive in its design and proficiency of execution that it has been attributed to one quilter, Mary Evans, possibly a protégée of Wilkins. Characteristics of her work include elaborate floral sprays, latticed baskets of flowers, and intricate depictions of hunting and harbor scenes, ships, trains, and Baltimore monuments, all popular quilt-block motifs. A professional quilter such as Mary Evans probably would take orders for an entire quilt as well as for blocks to be sold separately to accompany other homemade squares (Katzenburg 1981, 62).

Quilt, Pecolia Warner, Mississippi.

Though the popularity of the Album Quilt reached its peak in Baltimore, it was fashionable all over the country. A striking example comes from Alabama. According to family history, this quilt was made by the ladies of Greene and Hale counties and presented to Mr. Lewis Lanford in 1872 in appreciation of his untiring efforts in protecting them during the Reconstruction era. Sometimes the number of stars included in a flag gives a clue to its date. This flag, however, bears thirty stars, indicating a date between 1850 and 1858, which conflicts with the oral history. The 1880 census tends to support the family history, listing Lewis Lanford of Greene County as a farmer born in Alabama in 1844.

Another example of an album design, never assembled into a quilt but lovingly placed in a "Friendship Quilt Book," had blocks made by the Saxon family of South Carolina and Georgia between 1852 and 1855. There were fifteen blocks approximately sixteen inches square and one larger block

Friendship quilt, North Carolina.

thirty-three inches square. Judging by the inscription, the project was probably intended for presentation to the quilters' grandmother:

Pieced and appliquéd quilt,
South Carolina.

> This pleasing task I undertake;
> With fondness and delight,
> And as it is for Grandma's sake
> I'll work with all my might;
> With fond affection I will give,
> This patch in colours, bright
>
> And hope you may forever live;
> Where all is love and light.

And the large central block:

> And while my soul retains the power
> To think upon each faded year,
> In every bright or shadowed hour,
> My heart shall hold my mother dear.

L. V. Saxon
August 30, 1854

Geometric patchwork dominated quilt styles in the nineteenth century, especially from the 1830s onward. Through judicious choice of color and shape, dramatic and artistic quilts were created. Also popular were quilts influenced by the decorative style of the Victorian era. Quilts were used in the parlor as throws or lap robes, or to cover the piano or sofa. Under the Victorian influence, opulent silks and velvets replaced the colorful calicoes of the previous decades. Incorporated into these pieces were ribbons, beads, painted designs, and elaborately embroidered figures. Many quilts exhibited a high degree of originality and often included the signature of the quilter, date of completion, and names of family members.

Enthusiasm for quilt making ebbed near the end of the nineteenth century, but it became a popular pastime again during the Great Depression.

193

Commemorative quilt, Mobile.

Quilt, Pecolia Warner, Mississippi.

Appliquéd quilt, North Carolina.

Quilt making provided a creative outlet, perhaps a temporary reprieve from the despair of the day, and also produced an object of utility and beauty. Once again, old and new patterns for quilts appeared everywhere, especially in newspapers, farm journals, and ladies' magazines. Designs based on new technology, such as the airplane, were popular as well as the traditional "Fan" and "Dresden Plate" patterns, which were updated in an Art Deco style, and flower designs, of which *Morning Glories* is an example.

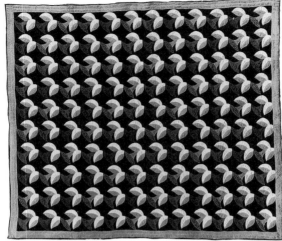

Morning Glories quilt, Alabama.

Recent research has provided valuable information on Afro-American quilts, a previously little-recognized American textile tradition. The natives of West and Central Africa who arrived in America between 1650 and 1850 brought with them a strong textile heritage. The Anglo-American techniques of piecing, appliquéing, and quilting were known and practiced in Africa, but the African interpretation of these techniques created dramatically different quilts.

Though not common in Africa, quilting was found among the people of the southern Saharan region. Here, quilts were used not for warmth but for protection. Quilted armor was made for both the warrior and his horse in this historically unsettled area (Picton and Mack 1979, 9–15, 169–81; Vlach 1978, 43–67). The African techniques and designs were subtly integrated into the Anglo-American tradition of creating bedcovers.

Piecing in strips, bright colors, large designs, asymmetry, and improvisation are characteristic of Afro-American quilts. Throughout West Africa, men wove cloth on narrow looms, making long strips of cloth which were pieced together to form a larger textile. The strip quilt, a dominant Afro-American pattern, was undoubtedly influenced by these narrow weaving looms. The quilt tops were asymmetrical and seemingly random in design, varying greatly from the orderly, repetitive block pattern of most nineteenth-century Anglo-American quilts.

Wall hangings which told a story in pictures, especially common in Ghana and Dahomey, were made from cutout shapes applied to a ground fabric. Appliquéd cloths designed to tell a story or record an event were also an important West African textile tradition. The most famous of all Afro-American quilts were two appliquéd quilts made by Harriet Powers (1837–1911) in 1886 and 1898. These quilts illustrate biblical scenes as well as local events and legends and are the only known examples of her extraordinary talent.

195

Pictorial quilt, Harriet Powers.

Mrs. Harriet Powers, nineteenth century.

Pictorial Bible quilt, Harriet Powers.

197

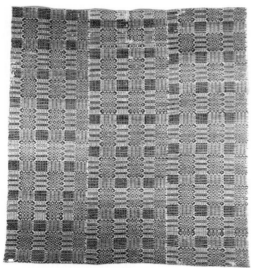

Overshot coverlet, Georgia.

Powers was born a slave in Georgia. She was probably taught quilting on the Georgia plantation but learned the African appliqué style from her parents or older slaves. While her themes were based on Western biblical sources, Powers's style showed a close affinity with African works. Needing money, she was forced to sell her first quilt in 1891 to Jennie Smith, an artist and art teacher at the Lucy Cobb School in Athens, Georgia. Powers gave Miss Smith a full description of each scene, which has been preserved. Impressed by the work's creativity and skill, Smith exhibited the quilt in the Negro Building at the Cotton States and International Exposition of 1895 in Atlanta. Presumably it was seen and admired by the wives of Atlanta University professors, and this resulted in a commission by the professors' wives for the second quilt as a presentation piece for the Reverend Charles Cuthbert Hall, Chairman of the Board of Trustees of the University.

Many examples of a very fine type of needlework, the all-white quilt, were found in the South; the warmer climate perhaps fostered the lighter, cooler bedcovering. The minute and subtle stitching on these quilts was so fine that many examples contained over a million stitches. The all-white quilts were produced by only the most accomplished needlewomen. The foundation fabric was usually cotton or linen in a plain weave. The backing was a similar cloth, though usually a coarser weave. The interlining was thin enough to allow even the most delicate quilting. Especially popular design motifs included urns, swags, and stylized flowers derived from the classical revival of the mid- to late 1800s which greatly influenced American art and architecture of the period.

The quilter could choose one of a number of techniques to join the quilt layers. Among those available were quilting, cording, stuffing, embroidering, and candlewicking. Quilting was executed using tiny stitches which created a stippled effect. There were two methods of cording: the quilter made very narrow rows of running stitches to form channels through which a yarn could be drawn; or, in a second method, the design was drawn on top of the backing fabric, the yarn was tacked down along the design, the top was laid down, and the two were quilted together. Like cording, the technique of stuffing created a raised design on the surface of the bedcovering. The quilter separated the loosely woven threads of the backing fabric and forced bits of cotton into the quilted outline of a flower, bunch of grapes, or other design.

198

The threads were then scratched together to seal the opening. One outstanding quilt titled *A Representation of the Fair Ground Near Russellville, Kentucky* demonstrates examples of all three techniques: quilting, cording, and stuffing. There are approximately 150 stitches in every square inch of the quilt for a total of 1,200,600 stitches (Orlofsky and Orlofsky 1974, 187–88). In the center of the quilt is the judging ring with a parade of horses, farm animals, and people, surrounded by elaborately detailed figures of trees and flowers and people in buggies and on horses. The quilt was made by Virginia Ivey in 1856, presumably to commemorate her visit to the fair.

Embroidery in white wool or cotton was a popular technique used frequently on white bedcovers. A good example of the embroidered bedcover was one made by Nancy Christian in 1818, who used basic embroidery stitches including French knots; chain, satin, and stem stitch; and couching.

A white bedcover embroidered with white roving (a twisted strand of fibers) was often referred to as a *candlewick* spread. Candlewicking was executed with the loosely spun yarn used as a wick in candles. Sometimes these bedcovers were tufted; using large, running stitches, the wicking was worked in the cover, leaving loops of thread on top which were then cut. When the piece was washed, the tufts pulled tight and were fluffed to form the design. Jemima Ann Beall-Hammond's candlewick spread is a good example of tufting.

Though women were responsible for furnishing cloth for their homes and households, it is unclear whether most of the cloth was produced within the home or purchased from professional weavers and merchants. Certainly the colonial mistress in the settled communities did not generally spin and weave the clothing for her family, since large quantities of manufactured goods were purchased from London. However, the war with England and the migration westward created a need for greater self-sufficiency, and the laborious task of producing cotton and linen cloth was borne by the housewife. Commercially produced cloth was available in the nineteenth century, though it was usually simple in construction and used for sacking, slaves' clothing, or coarse bedding.

Joining the housewife and factory in textile production was the professional weaver. Scant documentation exists on the professional weaver in the South. The weaver performed custom work, and the spun cotton thread and

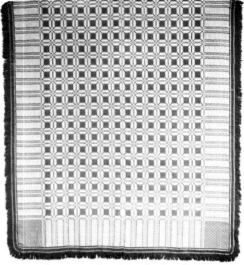

Overshot coverlet, North Carolina.

Whitework bedcover,
Sarah B. Wisdom, Virginia.

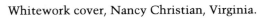
Whitework cover, Nancy Christian, Virginia.

Candlewick bedspread, Jemima Ann Beall-Hammond, Maryland.

Wool and wool and linen blankets, ca. 1800–1900.

woolen yarns were generally provided by the customer. Professionals often dyed the yarns, though this was a task assumed by many housewives.

Handloomed coverlets were popular in both the South and North; the most common type was the overshot coverlet. Construction involved a supplementary weft, usually cotton, which overshot the foundation weave, usually a cotton warp (threads that run vertically on the loom) and wool weft (threads that run horizontally), to form a geometric pattern and create a raised effect. A handloom with four harnesses (used to guide the warp threads) was needed for the coverlet construction.

Summer-and-winter, multiple shaft, double cloth, and Beiderwand were also types of coverlets that were handloomed (Davison and Mayer-Thurman 1973, 18). Summer-and-winter and multiple shaft were descriptive names and did not refer to the actual construction of the coverlet. Summer-and-winter, a term used in America from at least the nineteenth century, probably referred to the dark and light sides of the coverlet, the dark side being used during the winter and its reverse during the summer. Multiple-shaft coverlets required a loom with more than four harnesses for their patterning. Overshot, double cloth, and Beiderwand did refer to the method of coverlet construction. For double-cloth construction, two layers of fabric were produced simultaneously, with the weaver using two sets of warp and two sets of weft threads. Beiderwand, the name of an eighteenth-century German double-woven cloth, described the coverlet's compound weave structure which was characterized by a ribbed surface texture.

A Jacquard attachment mounted on a handloom offered an alternative to the geometric patterns of the common handloomed coverlet. The Jacquard attachment enabled weavers to create pictorial designs by means of prepunched pattern cards. Joseph-Marie Jacquard (1752–1834) perfected this loom apparatus in the early nineteenth century. It was introduced into the United States by the Horstman Company of Philadelphia about 1824. Trained weavers were required to operate the complicated and costly Jacquard attachment. Numerous guild-trained European weavers came to America seeking this type of work and settled in small towns as community weavers. Most seemed to settle in the Northeast and Midwest. Though a number of weavers worked in Maryland, and a few in West Virginia, Kentucky, and Tennessee, few Jacquard coverlets were made in the South (Heisey, Andrews, and Walters 1978, 10; Hulan 1971, 386–87). The pictorial

Mrs. Finley Mast weaving, 1914 photograph.

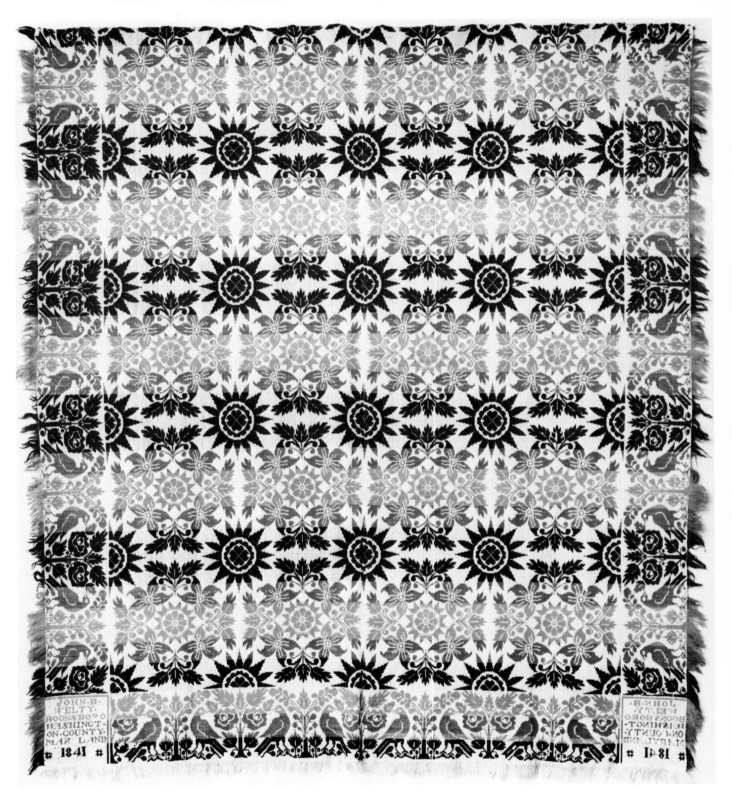

Jacquard coverlet, John B. Welty, Maryland.

nature of these coverlets made them very exciting visually. The weaver often signed his name, date, and place of execution in the corner block, though the client's name was sometimes woven there, creating complications when attempting to record and document the coverlet makers.

The most frequently used fabric dyes in America were extracted from plant or animal materials. Indigo was used for blue and madder or cochineal for red. Madder and cochineal, however, were not native to America and had to be imported. Additional plant materials which were raised locally for dyes expanded the weaver's options in color selection. In 1856, an Englishman, William Henry Perkins, discovered a lavender dye made from aniline. The popularity of this commercial dye hastened the end of the use of natural dyes in the 1860s and 1870s and launched a synthetic dye industry that produced a new, wide range of colors.

The weaver's patterns were as essential as the materials and loom. They gave instructions for the warping of the loom and construction of the fabric to be woven. The patterns were treated with special care and were often handed down in the family like treasured recipes. Though patterns did have specific names, they often varied from region to region, and the same pattern might have been known by more than one name. To add to the confusion, quilt and coverlet names were sometimes interchanged, making it very difficult to ascribe only one name to a particular pattern.

The bed rug was the rarest form of bedcovering. Until about 1820, "rugg" referred to a woolen cloth or bedcover. Most of the "ruggs" made and used by Americans in the eighteenth and early nineteenth centuries covered beds and furniture, not floors. Though more common in New England, bed rugs were used in eighteenth-century Southern interiors as well. They are mentioned in estate inventories in the eighteenth and early nineteenth centuries, though few are found today. A bed rug from the John Marshall house in Richmond, Virginia, was made between 1770 and 1820. The foundation was made of natural, unbleached wool, and the decoration was worked with embroidered knots of wool. Bed rugs commonly had bold designs which were probably inspired by English and East Indian textiles.

In most early-nineteenth-century homes, the floors were kept bare. Often sand, which would absorb grease and dirt, covered the kitchen and parlor floors and was brushed into decorative patterns with a broom. Later,

Bed rug, Virginia, 1770–1820.

Shaker horse rug, Shakertown at Pleasant Hill, Kentucky.

Shaker rug, Shakertown at Pleasant Hill, Kentucky.

however, a variety of rugs were introduced which offered warmth and ornamentation to the house. Yarn-sewn, hooked, shirred, and braided rugs could be made at home, usually from scraps of leftover fabric, and were fashioned in a wide variety of delightful pictorial and geometric designs.

Some of the most engaging hooked and shirred rugs were produced in the Shaker community of Pleasant Hill, Kentucky. A hooked rug was made by drawing yarn or strips of cloth through a backing with a hook which created a raised surface on the face of the rug. For a shirred rug, strips of fabric were folded in half, sewn, and pulled tight to create shirred or ruffled pieces which were then sewn onto a backing. Most of the Shaker rugs did not have pictorial images since representational art was discouraged. However, the creator of a rug from Pleasant Hill seems to have been influenced by the nearby horse farms of Lexington. The rug has a central design of a horse framed by a series of decorative borders, scallops, rectangles, and triangles. Some examples have floral designs, though the majority have geometric patterns. In one rug the word "good" is spelled out, and hearts are used liberally inside other shapes. Most of the Shaker rugs were made during the latter part of the nineteenth century.

Another Shaker industry in Kentucky was silk culture, a business which flourished between 1825 and 1875. A visitor to Pleasant Hill, Kentucky, reported in 1825 that the silkworm was raised there and that "sewing silk of superior quality is made of its web" (Neal 1974, 610). Beautiful silk kerchiefs were made from these silks. The men's neckerchiefs were collar width, fastened in the back, and had a small bow in front. The women's were rectangular in shape and were worn around the shoulders. The silks were characterized by fine weaving, rich colors, and beautifully blended, often iridescent, shades. Colors included blue, white, pink, mulberry, and shades of brown and purple. Some of the pieces were checked; others had contrasting borders. Many of the kerchiefs were sold or sent as gifts to the Shaker communities in the East.

Women played a significant role in the development of the silk industry in America, especially in Virginia, South Carolina, and Georgia. Promoters trying to encourage colonization of Georgia appealed to the poorer classes in England by promising them that women and children would find employment in the silk industry: "Let him see the People all in Employment of various Kinds, Women and Children feeding and nursing Silkworms, winding off the Silk . . ." (Spruill [1938] 1972, 16). And almost a century later, a Georgia woman who raised silkworms said she could sell as much as she could weave to South Carolinians at double the price of French or English silks. She said, "The people of South Carolina were all for living on their own resources, and having no dependence on other countries they, therefore, readily paid double prices for silks grown and manufactured at home, because it shut out the foreign trader, and kept all the money in the country." (Buckingham [1842, 1:162–64] McKissick 1932).

Rarely is an example of a truly regional textile tradition found in America. But recent research centering at the Louisiana State Museum in New Orleans has shed light on the textile tradition of the Louisiana Acadians. The Acadians immigrated to Louisiana after being expelled from Canada by the British when they remained loyal to France after the Seven Years' War (1756–1763). They settled in an isolated area along the coast of Louisiana (now Saint John the Baptist, Saint James, and Ascension parishes along the Mississippi River), where they were separated from outside cultural influences and urbanization.

Acadians produced their own cloth for use within the home or community from the time of their migration south to the first quarter of the twentieth century. Their isolation, coupled with an economy that was based more on barter than cash, limited the availability of imported fabrics and raw materials and fostered the continuation of the weaving tradition into the twentieth century. Their fabrics were simple and were constructed mostly of cotton on two-harness looms in a limited range of colors.

The predominant colors of the textiles were blue, brown, and white. The Acadians cultivated brown as well as white cotton. Its color offered an attractive variation at a time when dyeing cotton was difficult. Indigo, which was grown in Louisiana, was used by the Acadians along with a few other natural dyes.

Acadian weavers introduced strands of heavier yarn into the warp or weft of their cloth, creating a ribbed or tufted texture. Using the same technique, the weaver could add a different color yarn, either singly or plied with the ground color, to form a heavier yarn twisted in a spiral pattern. This gave almost endless variation to the warp and weft thread patterns, creating some

Acadian whitework or *courte-pointe* bedspread made by Lorita Macca.

Madame Dronet at her loom, 1938.

strikingly beautiful fabrics within the confines of two-harness weaving and a limited palette. These weaving techniques continued to survive well into the 1930s, supported by a growing interest by some prominent Louisiana citizens in their folk culture.

The tradition of creating textiles for home and family has been passed from mother to child for generations. Styles change, new fabrics and techniques are introduced, yet the tradition continues. Utility and necessity are strong motivators. However, the joy each artist receives from her or his personal expression insures the survival of various textile techniques.

Traditional styles and techniques continued for a longer period in the South than in the North. The South, in general, remained more rural, more isolated, and more dependent on local manufacture. In addition the South, for obvious reasons, became more aware of itself as a distinct part of the country after 1860 and began to view itself through new eyes and with a new perspective. In the later nineteenth and early twentieth centuries, Southern artists, craftsmen, and writers began to work with the knowledge of this distinction, ever aware of their very special "sense of place." While this regional imagery is only seldom expressed in textiles, its spirit is a part of every object.

Gail Andrews Trechsel
Birmingham Museum of Art

Silk kerchiefs from South Union Shaker Community.

Acknowledgments

So many people helped me during the preparation of *Southern Folk Art* that it is difficult to express my profound appreciation. My first and biggest thank you is to Dr. Robert Bishop, Director of the Museum of American Folk Art, who encouraged me and supported this exhibition and book from the beginning; next, to Dr. R. Lewis Wright, who shared his knowledge of Virginia artists and folk art; to Sarah Wright, a gracious hostess; to Howard Smith, who logged thousands of miles with me; to Ann Smith; to Rob Hicklin; to Terry Zug, one of my original Southern contacts; to Judy Peiser, for her hospitality; to Larry Harwell, photographer "extraordinaire"; to the people at the Museum of Early Southern Decorative Arts: Luke Beckerdite, John Bivins, Jr., Rosemary Estes, Sara Lee Frizzell, Sally Gant, Carolyn Head, Frank L. Horton, Audrey Michie, Elizabeth Putney, Brad Rauschenberg, and Paula Young; to Marianne Woods; to Carlton Palmer, photographer for the Museum of American Folk Art; to Gerry Werkin, Assistant Director of the Museum of American Folk Art; to Professor Steven Stowe; to Jean Lipman; and special thanks to Felicia Eth.

To everyone at the Museum of American Folk Art, I express warm appreciation; each person worked in some way to insure the success of this exhibition and book. I thank Clifford LaFontaine and his staff for a memorable installation. I am also grateful to the people at Philip Morris, Inc., especially Stephanie French and Karen Brosius, for providing me with the opportunity of working with them and for helping *Southern Folk Art* reach a wide audience.

Finally, I thank the following experts, colleagues, and collectors who gave their time, knowledge, and often their hospitality to make this exhibition and book a lasting contribution to the field of American folk art:

Barbara Luck, Beatrix Rumford, and Carolyn Weekley—*Abby Aldrich Rockefeller Folk Art Center*; Wanda Calhoon and Dean Walker—*Ackland Art Museum*; Bob Cason—*Alabama Department of Archives and History*; Hank Willet—*Alabama State Council for the Arts and Humanities*; Edmund Berkeley, Jr. and Greg Johnson—*Alderman Library of the University of Virginia*; Jimmy Allen; H. Parrott Bacot—*Anglo-American Art Museum*; Carol Hotchkiss-Malt—*Art and Culture Center of Hollywood, Florida*; Flossie Asher; Stephenson Andrews—*Association for the Preservation of Virginia Antiquities*; Elaine Kirkland, John Ott, and Michael Rose—*Atlanta Historical Society*; Barbara Bailey; Dena Katzenberg and Nancy Press—*Baltimore Museum of Art*; Bryding Adams Henley and Gail Andrews Trechsel—*Birmingham Museum of Art*; Joan Bluethenthal; Tim Bookout; Daisy Wade Bridges; John Burrison; Mrs. Charles Bybee; Dr. Benjamin Caldwell; Robert and Helen Cargo; Jan Hiester—*Charleston Museum*; Linda Chesnut; Dr. H. E. Comstock; Rebecca Tiger—*Cocoran Gallery of Art*; Charles Seeman—*Country Music Foundation*; Dr. Henry Deyerle; Ralph Esmerian; Terry Ferrell; Rick Bell and James Holmberg—*Filson Club*; Mary Victor—*Fine Arts Museum of the South*; Mrs. John Napier III and Virginia Richardson—*First White House of the Confederacy*; Abby and B. H. Friedman; Damon Hickey—

A Full View of Deadrick's Hill, Rebecca Chester.

Friends Historical Collection of Guilford College; Robert Gallimore; Sidney Gecker; Dr. Arthur Goldberg; Barbara Grabhorn; James A. Brewer—*Grand Lodge of Virginia A. F. and A. M.*; Karen C. Carroll—*Greensboro Historical Museum*; Dr. Georgeanna Greer; Gwen and Rob Griffin; Cheri Harrison and Charles Hilburn—*Gulf States Paper Corporation*; Barbara Brand—*Hammond-Harwood House*; Mrs. William Randolph Hearst, Jr.; Herbert W. Hemphill, Jr.; Walter E. Simmons II—*Henry Ford Museum and Greenfield Village*; Elizabeth Bachetti and Donald Peirce—*High Museum of Art*; Stanton Frazar, John A. Mahé II, Pat McWhorter, and Michele Wyckoff—*Historic New Orleans Collection*; Dr. John and Joyce Hoar; Jonathan Holstein; G. Eason Eige—*Huntingdon Galleries*; John Rice Irwin; Georgine Clark—*Kentucky-Alabama Crafts Council*; Frank Padgett—*Kentucky Department of the Arts*; Elizabeth Perkins, Charles Pittenger, and Catherine Zwyer—*Kentucky History Museum*; Hannelis Kuntze; Carolyn King and Mary Ann Neeley—*Landmarks Foundation of Montgomery*; Helen and Nell Laughon; Deanne Levison; Lynn Nanney—*Liberty Corporation*; Charles de la Gueronnière, Burt Harter, Maud Lyon, and Robert Macdonald—*Louisiana State Museum*; Patricia Hobbs and Thomas G. Ledford—*Lynchburg Museum System*; V. A. Patterson—*Manship House*; Chilton McDonnell; Catherine Horne and George Terry—*McKissick Museums*; Phil Meyers; Milton Block, Pamela Daniel, Charles Mo, and Stuart C. Schwartz—*Mint Museum*; Tish Haas and George Williams—*Mississippi Department of Economic Development*; Margaret Brown—*Mississippi Governor's Mansion*; Judy Shute—*Mississippi Restaurant Association*; Patti Carr Black and Mary Lohrenz—*Mississippi State Historical Museum*; J. Roderick and Sally Moore; Blanche W. Moss; Jan Clement—*Mud Island Mississippi River Museum*; Bridget A. Power—*Museum of Fine Arts*; Dennis Pullen—*Museum of Florida History*; Caldwell Delaney—*Museums of the City of Mobile*; Rita Adrosko, Richard Ahlborn, Doris Bowman, and Alice McHinney—*National Museum of American History*; Mr. and Mrs. Ralph Newsome; Catherine Warwick and Laurie Weitzenkorn—*National Gallery of Art*; Patricia Geeson—*National Museum of American Art*; Bill Fagaly—*New Orleans Museum of Art*; Donald Anderle—*New York Public Library*; Joe Nicholson; Jolene Greenwell and Alice Heaton—*Office of Historic Properties for Kentucky*; Mary Jo Thompson—*Old Governor's Mansion, Milledgeville, Georgia*; Paula Locklair—*Old Salem, Inc.*; Mr. and Mrs. George Overstreet; Bobbye J. Porter; Sumpter Priddy III; Burton and Kathleen Purmell; James M. Koenig—*Renfrew Museum and Park*; Harry M. Rhett, Jr.; Betty Ring; Susan Roach-Lankford; John Dutton—*Rural Life Museum*; Cecilia Steinfeldt—*San Antonio Museum Association*; Joan Selfe; Ed Nichols and James Thomas—*Shakertown at Pleasant Hill*; John Campbell—*Shakertown at South Union*; Tony and Marie Shank; Hilda Sexton—*Shorter Mansion Museum*; Sister Aloysia Dugan—*Sisters of Charity, Emmitsburg, Maryland*; Larry Southworth; Mary Carver and Jessie Wright—*J. B. Speed Art Museum*; Ryan Smith—*Star of Republic Museum*; Samuel Smith—*Tennessee Department of Conservation*; Stephen Cox, John Frase, and Dr. Jim Kelly—*Tennessee State Museum*; Betty Dillard—*Texas Homes Magazine*; Anne Dingus—*Texas Monthly Magazine*; Ella King Torrey; Mr. and Mrs. William Trotter; Robert Willingham, Jr.—*University of Georgia Libraries*; Clarita Anderson—*University of Maryland, Department of Textiles*; Gloria Jaster—*University of Texas at Austin, Winedale Historical Center*; Mr. and Mrs. Don Upchurch; Elizabeth Childs and Bruce King—*Valentine Museum*; Marjorie Peters—*Washington County Historical Center*; Dr. and Mrs. Franklin P. Watkins; Dr. and Mrs. George Waynick, Jr.; Vaughn Webb—*Blue Ridge Institute*; John Wells; Riley Handy—*Western Kentucky University, Kentucky Library*; Anne Wainstein—*West Virginia Department of Culture and History*; Derita Williams; James Arthur Williams; Karol Schmiegel and Frank A. Sommer—*Winterthur Museum*; Klaus and Monique Fong Wust; and Shelly Zegart.

Bibliography

General History

Bridenbaugh, Carl. *The Colonial Craftsman.* Chicago and London: University of Chicago Press, 1961.

————. *Myths and Realities: Societies of the Colonial South.* Louisiana State University Press, 1952. Reprint. New York: Atheneum, 1980.

Buckingham, J. S. *The Slave States of America.* 1842. Vol. 1, 163–64. Reprint. In "Some Observations of Travelers on South Carolina, 1820–1860," by J. Rion McKissick. *The Proceedings of the South Carolina Historical Association,* 1932.

Clinton, Catherine. *The Plantation Mistress: Women's World in the Old South.* New York: Pantheon Books, 1982.

Eaton, Clement. *A History of the Old South.* New York: Macmillan Co., 1949.

Howard, Robert West, ed. *This is the South.* Chicago: Rand McNally & Co., 1959.

Mitchell, Robert D. *Commercialism and Frontier: Perspectives on the Early Shenandoah Valley.* Charlottesville: University Press of Virginia, 1977.

Olmsted, Frederick Law. *A Journey in the Back Country.* Mason Brothers of New York, 1860. Reprint. New York: Schocken Books, 1970.

Spruill, Julia Cherry. *Woman's Life and Work in the Southern Colonies.* University of North Carolina Press, 1938. Reprint. New York and London: W. W. Norton & Co., 1972.

Wertenbaker, Thomas Jefferson. *The Old South: The Founding of American Civilization.* New York: Cooper Square Publishers, Inc., 1963.

General Folk Art

Albright, Frank P. "The Crafts of Salem." *The Magazine ANTIQUES* 88 (July 1965):94–97.

American Folk Art from the Abby Aldrich Rockefeller Folk Art Collection. Williamsburg: Colonial Williamsburg Foundation, 1959.

Bishop, Robert Charles. *American Folk Sculpture.* New York: E. P. Dutton & Co., Inc., 1974.

————. *Folk Painters of America.* New York: E. P. Dutton & Co., Inc., 1979.

Bishop, Robert Charles, and Patricia Coblentz. *A Gallery of American Weathervanes and Whirligigs.* New York: Bonanza Books, distributed by Crown, 1981.

Bishop, Robert Charles, and Carleton L. Safford. *America's Quilts and Coverlets.* New York: E. P. Dutton & Co., Inc., 1972.

Bivins, John, Jr. *Two Hundred Years of the Visual Arts in North Carolina: An Introduction to the Decorative Arts of North Carolina, 1776–1976.* Raleigh: North Carolina Museum of Art, 1976.

Bivins, John, Jr., and Paula Welshimer. *Moravian Decorative Arts in North Carolina: An Introduction to the Old Salem Collection.* Winston-Salem: Old Salem, Inc., 1981.

Black, Mary C., and Jean Lipman. *American Folk Painting.* New York: Clarkson N. Potter, 1966.

Brightman, Anna. "The Winedale Stagecoach Inn near Round Top, Texas." *The Magazine ANTIQUES* 94 (July 1968): 96–99.

Cahill, Holger. *American Folk Art: The Art of the Common Man in America, 1750–1900.* New York: Museum of Modern Art, 1932.

Christensen, Edwin O. *The Index of American Design.* Washington, D.C.: National Gallery of Art, 1950.

Davis, Chester. "The Moravians of Salem." *The Magazine ANTIQUES* 88 (July 1965): 60–64.

deCaro, F. A., and R. A. Jordan. *Louisiana Traditional Crafts.* Baton Rouge: LSU Union Gallery, Louisiana State University, 1980.

Doing It Right and Passing It On: North Louisiana Crafts. Alexandria: Alexandria Museum/Visual Art Center, 1981.

Ferris, William. *Local Color: A Sense of Place in Folk Art.* New York: McGraw-Hill Paperbacks, 1982.

Ferris, William, ed. *Afro-American Folk Art and Crafts.* Boston: G. K. Hall, Inc., 1982.

Folk Art in America: A Living Tradition. Selections from the Abby Aldrich Rockefeller Folk Art Collection. Atlanta: High Museum of Art, 1974.

Frontier America: The Far West. Boston: Museum of Fine Arts, 1975.

Gusler, Wallace B. "The Arts of Shenandoah County, Virginia, 1770–1825." *Journal of Early Southern Decorative Arts* 5 (November 1979): 8–10.

Hanes, Ralph P. "Old Salem." *The Magazine ANTIQUES* 88 (July 1965): 99.

Harris, Mrs. W. L. "A Southern Wedding Gift." *The Magazine ANTIQUES* 5 (February 1924): 71.

Hemphill, Herbert Waide, Jr. "Notes on Georgia Folk Art." In *Missing Pieces: Georgia Folk Art, 1770–1976,* 11–14. Atlanta: Georgia Council for the Arts and Humanities, 1976.

Hornung, Clarence P. *Treasury of American Design.* 2 vols. New York: Harry N. Abrams, Inc.,1972.

Hulan, Richard H. "Music in Tennessee." *The Magazine ANTIQUES* 100 (September 1971): 418–19.

Hulton, Paul. *The Work of Jacques le Moyne de Morgues: A Huguenot Artist in France, Florida, and England.* London: British Museum Publications, 1977.

Hvidt, Kristian, ed. *Von Reck's Voyage: Drawings and Journal of Philip Georg Friedrich Von Reck.* Savannah: Beehive Press, 1980.

"Life in Charleston." *The Magazine ANTIQUES* 37 (March 1940): 137–39.

Lipman, Jean. *American Folk Art in Wood, Metal, and Stone.* New York: Pantheon Books, 1948. Reprint. New York: Dover Publications, Inc., 1972.

212

——. *American Primitive Painting.* New York: Oxford University Press, 1942.

Lipman, Jean, and Alice Winchester. *The Flowering of American Folk Art, 1776–1876.* New York: Viking Press, in cooperation with Whitney Museum of American Art, 1974.

Little, Nina F. *Abby Aldrich Rockefeller Folk Art Collection.* Williamsburg: Colonial Williamsburg Foundation, 1958.

Lorant, Stefan, ed. *The New World: The First Pictures of America Made by John White and Jacques Le Moyne and Engraved by Theodore De Bry.* New York: Book Collectors Society, 1946.

Louisiana Folk Art. Baton Rouge: Anglo-American Art Museum, Louisiana State University, 1972.

Made By Hand: Mississippi Folk Art. Jackson: Mississippi Department of Archives and History, 1980.

Made in Tennessee: An Exhibition of Early Arts and Crafts. Nashville: The National Life and Accident Insurance Company and WSM, Inc., 1971.

Missing Pieces: Georgia Folk Art, 1770–1976. Atlanta: Georgia Council for the Arts and Humanities, 1976.

Moore, J. Roderick. "Folk Crafts." *Arts in Virginia* 12, no. 1 (Fall 1971): 22–29.

Morton, Robert. *Southern Antiques and Folk Art.* Birmingham: Oxmoor House, 1976.

The Museum of Early Southern Decorative Arts. Winston-Salem: Old Salem, Inc., 1979.

Nineteenth-Century Folk Painting: Our Spirited National Heritage. Storrs, Conn.: University of Connecticut, William Benton Museum of Art, 1973.

Odell, Scott. "Folk Instruments." *Arts in Virginia* 12, no. 1 (Fall 1971): 30–37.

One hundred one American Primitive Watercolors and Pastels from the Collection of Edgar William and Bernice Chrysler Garbisch. Washington, D.C.: National Gallery of Art, n.d.

One hundred one Masterpieces of American Primitive Painting from the Collection of Edgar William and Bernice Chrysler Garbisch. New York: American Federation of Arts, 1961. Reprint. New York: Doubleday & Co., 1962.

Poesch, Jessie. *The Art of the Old South: Painting, Sculpture, Architecture, and the Products of Craftsmen, 1560–1860.* New York: Alfred A. Knopf, 1983.

Rumford, Beatrix T., ed. *American Folk Portraits: Paintings and Drawings from the Abby Aldrich Rockefeller Folk Art Center.* Boston: New York Graphic Society, 1981.

Seibels, Eugenia, and Jo Anne McCormick. *Southern Folk Arts. The University Museums: McKissick Library, University of South Carolina.* Columbia: University of South Carolina, 1977.

Steinfeldt, Cecilia. "The Folk Art of Frontier Texas." *The Magazine ANTIQUES* 114 (December 1978): 1280–89.

——. *Texas Folk Art: One Hundred Fifty Years of the Southwestern Tradition.* Austin: Texas Monthly Press, 1981.

Stitt, Susan. *Museum of Early Southern Decorative Arts in Old Salem.* Winston-Salem: Museum of Early Southern Decorative Arts, 1970.

Stoudt, John Joseph. *Early Pennsylvania Arts and Crafts.* South Brunswick, N.J.: A. S. Barnes, 1964.

Taylor, Lonn. "The McGregor-Grimm House at Winedale, Texas." *The Magazine ANTIQUES* 108 (September 1975): 515–21.

Terry, George D., and Lynn Robertson Myers. *Southern Make the Southern Folk Heritage.* Columbia: McKissick Museums, 1981.

Treasures of American Folk Art: From the Collection of the Museum of
American Folk Art. Introduction and commentaries by Robert Charles Bishop. New York: Harry N. Abrams, Inc., 1979.

van Ravensway, Charles. "The Creole Arts and Crafts of Upper Louisiana." *Bulletin of the Missouri Historical Society* (April 1956): 213–48.

A Virginia Sampler: Eighteenth, Nineteenth, and Twentieth Century Folk Art. Roanoke: Roanoke Fine Arts Center, 1976.

The Watercolor Drawings of John White from the British Museum. Washington, D.C.: National Gallery of Art, 1965.

Wright, R. Lewis. "Carl Hambuck, Richmond Artist." *The Clarion* (Winter 1983/1984): 46–48.

——. "Key Baskets." *Journal of Early Southern Decorative Arts* 8 (May 1982): 49–61.

Wust, Klaus. *American Fraktur: Graphic Folk Art, 1745–1855.* New York: Pratt Institute, 1976.

——. "Folk Design." *Arts in Virginia* 12, no. 1 (Fall 1971): 38–43.

——. "Fraktur and the Virginia Germans." *Arts in Virginia* 15, no. 1 (Fall 1974): 2–11.

——. *Virginia Fraktur: Penmanship as Folk Art.* Edinburg, Va.: Shenandoah History, 1972.

Jug, John C. Avera.

Pottery

Auman, Dorothy Cole, and Charles G. Zug III. "Nine Generations of Potters: The Cole Family." *Southern Exposure* 5:2–3 (1977): 166–74.

Barka, Norman F., and Chris Sheridan. "The Yorktown Pottery Industry, Yorktown, Virginia." *Northeast Historical Archeology* 6 (1977): 21–32.

Bivins, John, Jr. *The Moravian Potters in North Carolina.* Chapel Hill: University of North Carolina Press, 1972.

Bridges, Daisy Wade, ed. "Potters of the Catawba Valley, North Carolina." *Journal of Studies. Ceramic Circle of Charlotte* 4, 1980.

Burbage, Beverly S. "The Remarkable Pottery of Charles Decker and His Sons." *The Tennessee Conservationist* 37 (November 1971): 6–11.

Burrison, John A. "Afro-American Folk Pottery in the South." *Southern Folklore Quarterly* 42 (1978): 175–99.

——. "Alkaline-Glazed Stoneware: A Deep-South Pottery Tradition." *Southern Folklore Quarterly* 39 (1975): 377–403.

——. *Brothers in Clay: The Story of Georgia Folk Pottery.* Athens: University of Georgia Press, 1983.

——. "Folk Pottery of Georgia." In *Missing Pieces: Georgia Folk Art, 1770–1976,* 24–29. Atlanta: Georgia Council for the Arts and Humanities, 1976.

——. *The Meaders Family of Mossy Creek: Eighty Years of North Georgia Folk Pottery.* Atlanta: Georgia State University Art Gallery, 1976.

Crawford, Jean. *Jugtown Pottery: History and Design.* Winston-Salem: John F. Blair, Pub., 1964.

Ferrell, Stephen T., and T. M. Ferrell. *Early Decorated Stoneware of the Edgefield District, South Carolina.* Greenville: Greenville County Museum of Art, 1976.

Greer, Georgeanna H. "Alkaline Glazes and Groundhog Kilns: Southern Pottery Traditions." *The Magazine ANTIQUES* 111 (April 1977): 768–73.

——. *American Stonewares: The Art and Craft of Utilitarian Potters.* Exton, Pa.: Schiffer Publishing Ltd., 1981.

——. "The Folk Pottery of Mississippi." In *Made by Hand: Mississippi Folk Art,* 45–54. Jackson: Mississippi Department of Archives and History, 1980.

——. "Groundhog Kilns—Rectangular American Kilns of the Nineteenth and Early Twentieth Centuries." *Northeast Historical Archeology* 6 (1977): 42–54.

Greer, Georgeanna H., and Harding Black. *The Meyer Family: Master Potters of Texas.* San Antonio: Trinity University Press, 1971.

Kaufman, Stanley A. *Heatwole and Suter Pottery.* Harrisonburg, Va.: Good Printers, 1978.

Moore, J. Roderick. "Earthenware Potters along the Great Road in Virginia and Tennessee." *The Magazine ANTIQUES* 124 (September 1983): 528–37.

Rauschenberg, Bradford L. " 'B. DuVal & Co. Richmond': A Newly Discovered Pottery." *Journal of Early Southern Decorative Arts* 4 (May 1978): 45–75.

Rice, A. H., and John Baer Stoudt. *The Shenandoah Pottery.* Strasburg, 1929. Reprint. Berryville, Va.: Virginia Book Co., 1974.

Rinzler, Ralph, and Robert Sayers. *The Meaders Family: North Georgia Potters.* Smithsonian Folklife Series, no. 1. Washington, D.C.: Smithsonian Institution Press, 1980.

Scarborough, Quincy. "Connecticut Influence on North Carolina Stoneware: The Webster School of Potters." *Journal of Early Southern Decorative Arts* 10 (May 1984): 14–74.

Schwartz, Stuart C. *North Carolina Pottery: A Bibliography.* Charlotte: Mint Museum of History, 1978.

Smith, Samuel D., and Stephen T. Rogers. *A Survey of Historic Pottery Making in Tennessee.* Research series no. 3. Nashville: Division of Archeology, Tennessee Department of Conservation, 1979.

"Southern Folk Pottery." In *Foxfire Eight,* edited by Eliot Wigginton and Margie Bennett, 71–384. New York: Anchor Press/Doubleday, 1984.

Sweezy, Nancy. *Raised in Clay: The Southern Pottery Tradition.* Washington, D.C.: Smithsonian Institution Press, 1984.

Vlach, John Michael. "Pottery." In *The Afro-American Tradition in Decorative Arts,* 76–96. Cleveland: Cleveland Museum of Art, 1978.

Watkins, C. Malcolm. "Ceramics in the Seventeenth-Century English Colonies." In *Arts of the Anglo-American Community in the Seventeenth Century,* Winterthur Conference Report 1974, edited by Ian M. G. Quimby, 275–99. Charlottesville: University of Virginia Press, 1975.

Whatley, L. McKay. "The Mount Shepherd Pottery: Correlating Archeology and History." *Journal of Early Southern Decorative Arts* 6 (May 1980): 21–57.

Willett, E. Henry, and Joey Brackner. *The Traditional Pottery of Alabama.* Montgomery: Montgomery Museum of Fine Arts, 1983.

Wiltshire, William E. *Folk Pottery of the Shenandoah Valley.* New York: E. P. Dutton & Co., Inc., 1975.

Zug, Charles G. III. "Jugtown Reborn: The North Carolina Folk Pottery in Transition." *Pioneer America Society Transactions* 3 (1980): 1–24.

——. *The Traditional Pottery of North Carolina.* Chapel Hill: Ackland Art Museum, 1980.

Portrait of Josephine Edmonds Horner.

Painting

Adams, E. Bryding. "Frederick Kemmelmeyer, Maryland Itinerant Artist." *The Magazine ANTIQUES* 125 (January 1984).

———. "John Drinker, Portrait Painter and Limner." *Journal of Early Southern Decorative Arts* 7 (November 1981): 14–29.

Batson, Whaley. "Charles Peale Polk, Gold Profiles on Glass." *Journal of Early Southern Decorative Arts* 3 (November 1977): 51–57.

Bivins, John, Jr. "*Fraktur* in the South: An Itinerant Artist." *Journal of Early Southern Decorative Arts* 1 (November 1975): 1–23.

Black, Mary. "Folk Painting." *Arts in Virginia* 12, no. 1 (Fall 1971): 6–15.

Carroll, Karen Cobb. *Windows to the Past: Primitive Watercolors from Guilford County, North Carolina, in the 1820s.* Greensboro: Greensboro Historical Museum, 1983.

An Exhibition of Portraits by Joshua Johnston. Baltimore: Peale Museum, 1948.

Horton, Frank L. "America's Earliest Woman Miniaturist." *Journal of Early Southern Decorative Arts* 5 (November 1979): 1–5.

Knox, Ella Prince, and David S. Bundy, comps. *Painting in the South: 1564–1980.* Essays by Donald B. Kuspit, Jessie J. Poesch, Linda Crocker Simmons, Rick Stewart, Carolyn J. Weekley. Richmond: Virginia Museum of Fine Arts, 1983.

Kolbe, John Christian, and Brent Holcomb. "*Fraktur* in the Dutch Fork Area of South Carolina." *The Journal of Early Southern Decorative Arts* 5 (November 1979): 36–51.

Middleton, Margaret Simons. *Henrietta Johnston of Charles Town, South Carolina: America's First Pastellist.* Columbia: University of South Carolina Press, 1966.

National Society of the Colonial Dames of America in the State of Alabama. *Alabama Portraits prior to 1870.* Mobile, 1969.

National Society of the Colonial Dames of America in the State of Georgia. *Early Georgia Portraits, 1715–1870.* Athens: University of Georgia Press, 1975.

National Society of the Colonial Dames of America in the State of Louisiana. *Louisiana Portraits.* New Orleans, 1975.

National Society of the Colonial Dames of America in the State of North Carolina. *The North Carolina Portrait Index, 1700–1860.* Compiled by Laura MacMillan. Chapel Hill: University of North Carolina Press, 1963.

O'Kelley, Mattie Lou. *From the Hills of Georgia: An Autobiography in Paintings.* Boston and Toronto: Atlantic Monthly Press Book/Little, Brown & Co., 1983.

O'Neal, William B. *Primitive into Painter: Life and Letters of John Toole.* Charlottesville: University of Virginia Press, 1960.

Pleasants, Jacob Hall. "Joshua Johnston, the First American Negro Portrait Painter." *Maryland Historical Society* 37 (June 1942): 1–39. Reprint. 1970.

Rutledge, Anna Wells. "William Henry Brown of Charleston." *The Magazine ANTIQUES* 60 (December 1951): 532–33.

Sargent, William R. "The Quarles Portraits: Susannah Nicholson, Painter (1804–1858)." Master's thesis, Marshall University, Huntington, West Virginia, 1978.

Simmons, Linda Crocker. *Charles Peale Polk, 1767–1822: A Limner and His Likenesses.* Washington, D.C.: Corcoran Gallery of Art, 1981.

———. *Jacob Frymire, American Limner.* Washington, D.C.: Corcoran Gallery of Art, 1975.

Walters, Donald R. "Jacob Strickler, Shenandoah County, Virginia, *Fraktur* Artist." *The Magazine ANTIQUES* 110 (September 1976): 536–43.

Weekley, Carolyn J. "Decorated Family Record Books from the Valley of Virginia." *Journal of Early Southern Decorative Arts* 7 (May 1981): 1–19.

Wright, R. Lewis. *Artists in Virginia before 1900.* Charlottesville: Virginia Historical Society, University Press of Virginia, 1983.

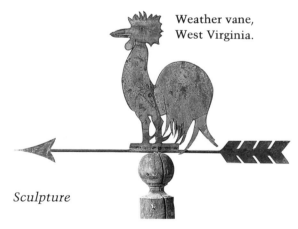

Weather vane, West Virginia.

Sculpture

Bridaham, Lester Burbank. "Pierre Joseph Landry, Louisiana Woodcarver." *The Magazine ANTIQUES* 72 (August 1957): 157–59.

Fleckenstein, Henry A., Jr. *Southern Decoys of Virginia and the Carolinas.* Exton, Pa.: Schiffer Publishing Ltd., 1983.

Fletcher, Georganne, ed. *William Edmondson: A Retrospective.* Nashville: Tennessee Arts Commission, 1981.

Fuller, Edmund L. *Visions in Stone: The Sculpture of William Edmondson.* Pittsburgh: University of Pittsburgh Press, 1973.

Haid, Alan G. *Decoys of the Mississippi Flyway.* Exton, Pa.: Schiffer Publishing Ltd., 1981.

Vlach, John Michael. "Blacksmithing." In *The Afro-American Tradition in Decorative Arts,* 108–21. Cleveland: Cleveland Museum of Art, 1978.

———. "Wood Carving." In *The Afro-American Tradition in Decorative Arts,* 27–43. Cleveland: Cleveland Museum of Art, 1978.

Wright, R. Lewis. "Sink Box Decoys: A Southern Art Form." *The Antiques Journal* (October 1981): 16–36.

Wust, Klaus. *Folk Art in Stone: Southwest Virginia.* Edinburg, Va.: Shenandoah History, 1970.

Close-up of applied hinge with tulip-motif terminal, Virginia.

Decorated Furniture

Beasley, Ellen. "Tennessee Cabinetmakers and Chairmakers through 1840." *The Magazine ANTIQUES* 100 (October 1971): 612–21.

Dockstader, Mary Ralls. "Sugar Chests." *The Magazine ANTIQUES* 25 (April 1934): 140–43.

Early French Louisiana Furnishings, 1700–1830. Text and catalog on furniture by Jack Holden. Text and catalog on weaving by Robert E. Smith. Lafayette: Art Center for Southwestern Louisiana, 1974.

Green, Henry D. *Furniture of the Georgia Piedmont before 1830.* Atlanta: High Museum of Art, 1976.

Moore, J. Roderick. "Painted Chests from Wythe County, Virginia." *The Magazine ANTIQUES* 122 (September 1982): 516–21.

———. "Wythe County, Virginia, Punched Tin: Its Influence and Imitators." *The Magazine ANTIQUES* 126 (September 1984): 601–13.

Neat Pieces: The Plain-Style Furniture of Nineteenth-Century Georgia. Atlanta: Atlanta Historical Society, 1983.

Piorkowski, Patricia A. *Piedmont Virginia Furniture.* Lynchburg: Lynchburg Fine Arts Center, 1982.

Poesch, Jessie J. *Early Furniture of Louisiana.* New Orleans: Louisiana State Museum, 1972.

———. "Early Louisiana Armoires." *The Magazine ANTIQUES* 94 (August 1968): 196–205.

———. "Furniture of the River Road Plantations in Louisiana." *The Magazine ANTIQUES* 111 (June 1977): 1184–93.

Swan, Mabel Munson. "Moravian Cabinetmakers." *The Magazine AN-TIQUES* 59 (June 1951): 456–59.

Taylor, Lonn, and David B. Warren. *Texas Furniture: The Cabinet-makers and Their Work, 1840–1880.* Austin: University of Texas Press, 1975.

Walters, Donald. "Johannes Spitler, Shenandoah County, Virginia, Furniture Decorator." *The Magazine ANTIQUES* 108 (October 1975): 730–35.

Wright, R. Lewis. "The Johnsons: Chairmaking in Mecklenburg County, Virginia." *Journal of Early Southern Decorative Arts* 6 (November 1980): 33–47.

Three painted, stippled, and stencilled boxes, Virginia.

Textiles

Adams, Dr. Monni. "Harriet Powers' Bible Quilts." *The Clarion* (Spring 1982): 36–43.

Anderson, Clarita. *"No Man Can Better It": Maryland Coverlets and Their Weavers.* College Park: University of Maryland, Department of Textiles and Consumer Economics, 1981.

Bespangled, Painted, and Embroidered Decorated Masonic Aprons in America, 1790–1850. Lexington, Mass.: Museum of Our National Heritage, 1980.

Black Belt to Hill Country: Alabama Quilts from the Robert and Helen Cargo Collection. Birmingham: Birmingham Museum of Art and the Alabama State Council on the Arts and Humanities, 1981.

Buckingham, J. S. *The Slave States of America.* 1842. Vol. 1, 163–64. Reprint. In "Some Observations of Travelers on South Carolina 1820–1860," by J. Rion McKissick. *The Proceedings of the South Carolina Historical Association,* 1932.

Bullard, Lacy Folmar, and Betty Jo Shiell. *Chintz Quilts: Unfading Glory.* Tallahassee: Serendipity Publishers, 1983.

Davis, Mildred J. "Textiles in the Valentine Museum." *The Magazine ANTIQUES* 103 (January 1973): 175–83.

Davison, Mildred, and Christa C. Mayer-Thurman. *Coverlets: A Handbook on the Collection of Woven Coverlets in the Art Institute of Chicago.* Chicago: Art Institute of Chicago, 1973.

Fry, Dr. Gladys-Marie. "Harriet Powers: Portrait of a Black Quilter." In *Missing Pieces: Georgia Folk Art, 1770–1976,* 17–23. Atlanta: Georgia Council for the Arts and Humanities, 1976.

Taufschein, Peter Bernhart.

Garrett, Elisabeth Donaghy. "American Samplers and Needlework Pictures in the DAR Museum. Part 1: 1739–1806." *The Magazine ANTIQUES* 105 (February 1974): 356–64.

———. "American Samplers and Needlework Pictures in the DAR Museum. Part 11: 1806–1840." *The Magazine ANTIQUES* 107 (April 1975): 688–701.

Gary, Virginia Gearhart. "Activities of Southern Women, 1840–60." *South Atlantic Quarterly* 2, 1928.

Glasgow, Vaughn L. "Textiles of the Louisiana Acadians." *The Magazine ANTIQUES* 100 (August 1981): 338–48.

Gordon, Beverly. *Shaker Textile Arts.* Hanover, N.H.: University Press of New England, 1980.

Heisey, John W., Gail C. Andrews, and Donald R. Walters. *A Checklist of American Coverlet Weavers.* Williamsburg: Colonial Williamsburg Foundation, 1978.

Hulan, Richard H. "Tennessee Textiles." *The Magazine ANTIQUES* 100 (September 1971): 386–89.

Irwin, John Rice. *A People and Their Quilts.* Exton, Pa.: Schiffer Publishing Ltd., 1983.

Katzenberg, Dena S. *Baltimore Album Quilts.* Baltimore: Baltimore Museum of Art, 1980.

"Kentuckiana Folk Weaving from Our Heritage to Contemporary Trends." *Kentucky Weaver* 8, no. 1. Louisville: Little Loomhouse of Lou Tate, 1955.

Kentucky Quilts, 1800–1900: The Kentucky Quilt Project. Introduction and quilt commentaries by Jonathan Holstein. Text by John Finley. Louisville: Kentucky Quilt Project, 1982. Reprint. New York: Pantheon Books, 1983.

L'Amour de Maman: La Tradition Acadienne du Tissage en Louisiane. La Rochelle: Musée du Nouveau Monde, 1983.

Mohamed, Ethel Wright. *My Life in Pictures.* Edited by Charlotte Capers and Olivia P. Collins. Jackson: Mississippi Department of Archives and History, 1976.

Montgomery, Florence M. *Printed Textiles: English and American Cottons and Linens, 1700–1850.* New York: A Winterthur Book, Viking Press, 1970.

Neal, Julia. "Shaker Industries in Kentucky," *The Magazine ANTIQUES* 105 (March 1974): 603–611.

North Carolina Country Quilts: Regional Variations. Chapel Hill: Ackland Art Museum, 1979.

Orlofsky, Patsy, and Myron Orlofsky. *Quilts in America.* New York: McGraw-Hill Book Co., 1974.

Picton, John, and John Mack. *African Textiles.* London: British Museum Publications Ltd., 1979.

Poesch, Jessie. *The Art of the Old South: Painting, Sculpture, Architecture, and the Products of Craftsmen, 1560–1860.* New York: Alfred A. Knopf, 1983.

Reynolds, Elizabeth. *Southern Comfort: Quilts from the Atlanta Historical Society.* Atlanta: Atlanta Historical Society, 1978.

Ring, Betty. "For Persons of Fortune Who Have Taste: An Elegant Schoolgirl Embroidery." *Journal of Early Southern Decorative Arts* 3, no. 2 (November 1977): 1–23.

———. "Memorial Embroideries by American Schoolgirls." *The Magazine ANTIQUES* 100 (October 1971): 570–75.

———. "Saint Joseph's Academy in Needlework Pictures." *The Magazine ANTIQUES* 113 (March 1978): 592–99.

Rossetter, Tabitha Wilson. "The Acadian Textile Heritage." *Fiberarts* (May/June 1981): 29–32.

Something to Keep You Warm: The Roland Freeman Collection of Black American Quilts from the Mississippi Heartland. Jackson: Mississippi Department of Archives and History, 1981.

Spruill, Julia Cherry. *Woman's Life and Work in the Southern Colonies.* University of North Carolina Press, 1938. Reprint. New York and London: W. W. Norton & Co., 1972.

Swan, Susan Burrows. *A Winterthur Guide to American Needlework.* New York: Crown Publishers, Inc., 1976.

Tate, Lou. "Kentucky's Coverlets." *The Magazine ANTIQUES* 105 (April 1974): 901–905.

Tinkham, Sandra Shaffer. "A Southern Bed Rugg." *The Magazine ANTIQUES* 105 (June 1974): 1320–21.

Tuska, Miriam Gittleman. "Kentucky Quilts." *The Magazine ANTIQUES* 105 (April 1974): 784–90.

Vlach, John Michael. "Quilting." In *The Afro-American Tradition in Decorative Arts,* 44–75. Cleveland: Cleveland Museum of Art, 1978.

Wilson, Sadye Tune, and Doris Finch Kennedy. *Of Coverlets: The Legacies, the Weavers.* Nashville: Tunstede Press, 1983.

Catalog of Illustrations

216

Alabama *Gunboat Quilt.*

The Sacrifice of Isaac, Elizabeth Boush.

House and lot of Dr. G.R.B. Horner/Part of Warrenton, Va./House of Mrs. Alex. Campbell, Gustavus Richard Brown Horner.

page 106   *Left:* **Cane.** Maker unknown. West Virginia, ca. 1875. Unidentified wood, height 38″. *Right:* **Cane.** Maker unknown. Thomasville, Georgia, ca. 1875. Unidentified wood, height 34-1/2″. *Right, bottom:* **Cane.** Maker unknown. Virginia, ca. 1890. Unidentified wood, height 28-1/2″. All canes this page: Photography by Carlton Palmer. Collection of Herbert W. Hemphill, Jr.

page 107   **Cane.** Maker unknown. Georgia, ca. 1900. Unidentified wood, height 35-1/4″. Photography by Carlton Palmer. Collection of Herbert W. Hemphill, Jr.

page 108   *Man with a Snake.* Edgar Alexander McKillop, artist. Walnut with glass and bone or ivory. Height 22″. The Ackland Art Museum, The University of North Carolina at Chapel Hill, Ackland Fund. **Walking cane.** Artist unknown. Walking cane showing the 170 electoral votes given to James K. Polk in the presidential campaign of 1844 by states. Ornately carved, with a brass tip. Length 35-3/4″, diameter at top 1-5/16″. Tennessee Historical Society.

page 109   **Staff and box.** Artist unknown. Afro-American Odd Fellows Lodge Hall, Staunton, Virginia, twentieth century. Paint on wood. Photography by Larry Harwell. Moore collection.

pages 110 and 111   **Family room.** Collection of North Carolina decoys, ca. 1890–1940s, Currituck Sound area and its outerbanks. Swans from North Carolina, ca. 1920s–1930s. Photography by Larry Harwell. Courtesy of Gwen and Ron Griffin.

page 112   **Owl decoy.** Maker unknown. Roanoke County, Virginia, ca. 1900. Height 15-1/2″. Unidentified wood, paint, and metal. Used in cherry orchard to keep birds away. Photography by Katherine Wetzel. Courtesy of Dr. R. Lewis Wright. **Bear figure.** Attributed to Anthony W. Baecher. Winchester, Virginia, late nineteenth century. Manganese-dioxide glazed redware. Glass container in bear's head is for ink; pewter top hat is for holding pen points. Photography by Larry Harwell. Moore collection.

page 113   *Top, first three decoys, and second row, last three decoys:* **Collection** of factory-made and Louisiana decoys. Photography by Jim Bathie. Courtesy of John and Joyce Hoar. *Top, fourth decoy:* **Sink box decoy.** Canvasback duck, maker unknown. Eastern Shore of Virginia, ca. 1850–1934. Yellow pine and paint. Used to supplement the sink box once the weight was attained. Photography by Katherine Wetzel. Courtesy of Dr. R. Lewis Wright. *Top, second row, first decoy:* **Sink box decoy.** Maker unknown. Perrysville, Maryland, ca. 1850–1934. Cast iron and paint. Photography by Katherine Wetzel. Courtesy of Dr. R. Lewis Wright. *Right, middle:* **Animals.** Charles Pierce, maker. Galax, Virginia, ca. 1940. Paint on wood. Photography by Larry Harwell. Moore collection. *Right, bottom:* **Animal paper weights.** Cast iron, nineteenth century. Elephant attributed to Mossy Creek Iron Works, Augusta County, Virginia. Dog found in Shenandoah County, Virginia. Parrot found in Botetourt County, Virginia. Photography by Larry Harwell. Moore collection.

page 114   *Left:* **Doll.** Maker unknown. Found in North Carolina, ca. 1850–1860. Cloth and oil. Height 25″. Courtesy of the Mint Museum, History Department, Charlotte, North Carolina. *Right:* **Doll.** "Miss Chitty." Maker unknown. Salem, North Carolina, ca. 1890–1940s. Muslin, paint, wearing original clothes. Height 25″. Photography by Howard A. Smith. Courtesy of Dr. and Mrs. George E. Waynick, Jr.

page 115   **Doll.** Attributed to Maggie and Bessie Phohl. Salem, North Carolina, prior to 1880. Muslin, paint, wearing original clothes. Height 28″. Photography by Howard A. Smith. Courtesy of Dr. and Mrs. George E. Waynick, Jr.

page 116   **Dolls.** *Left:* Wooden doll found in Shenandoah County, Virginia; military buttons, 1848; paint on wood. *Right:* Cloth or rag doll found in Shenandoah County, Virginia, ca. 1920. Photography by Larry Harwell. Moore collection.

page 117   *Left:* **Doll.** Maker unknown. Jekyll Island, Georgia, ca. 1850.

Cloth, silk, and wood. Height 32″. Photography by Carlton Palmer. Courtesy of L. E. Southworth. *Right:* **Doll.** Cloth, clay, paint, and flax with newspaper stuffing. Photography by Larry Harwell. Moore collection.

page 118   *Left, top:* **Toy.** W. A. Smith, artist. Tacoma, Florida, 1882. Wood, cloth, and wire. Made as a birthday gift, this doll churns butter when crank is turned. Height 12″, length 6-3/4″, width 3-1/4″. Photography by the Museum of Florida History. Museum of Florida History, Division of Archives, History, and Records Management, Florida Department of State. *Left, bottom:* **Doll.** Maker unknown. Found in Charleston, South Carolina. Cloth and wood. Height 10″. Photography by Larry Harwell. Private collection. *Right:* **Doll.** Maker unknown. Nineteenth century. Cotton; dress of linsey-woolsey. Length 22″. Atlanta Historical Society.

page 119   **Wheel of Life.** Pierre Joseph Landry, artist. Near Plaquemine, Louisiana, 1834. This sculpture depicts the nine stages of man. Louisiana State Museum.

page 120   *Left:* *Self Portrait of Artist Observing Indian Maiden at Her Bath.* Pierre Joseph Landry, artist. Wood: magnolia, ca. 1825. Height 18-5/8″, length 14-7/8″. Courtesy of the New Orleans Museum of Art; gift of Mrs. Emile Kuntz and family. *Right:* **Wood carving.** Edgar Alexander McKillop, artist. Balfour, North Carolina, ca. 1928. Wood: walnut. Height 52″, width 13″, depth 18″. Collections of Greenfield Village and the Henry Ford Museum, Dearborn, Michigan; gift of Edgar Alexander McKillop; negative no. B26024.

page 121   **Close-up and full view of statue of George Washington.** Captain Matthew S. Kahle, cabinetmaker, 1840. Courtesy, Washington and Lee University, Lexington, Virginia.

page 122   *Left:* **Church chandelier.** Luther Goins, artist. Maryland, ca. 1895. Poplar and pine. Height 39-1/2″, width 39″. Photograph courtesy of E. P. Dutton & Co., Inc. National Museum of American History, Smithsonian Institution. *Middle:* **Hand of God.** Artist unknown. Midway, Georgia, ca. 1895. Wood and white paint. Height 50″. Originally the steeple ornament for the Midway Temple Presbyterian Church. Photograph courtesy of E. P. Dutton & Co., Inc. Midway Museum. *Right:* **Carved head.** Artist unknown. Poplar, 1900–1920. Found in northeastern Tennessee. Photography by Larry Harwell. Private collection.

page 123   **Steamboat model** of the side-wheeler *Globe.* A. C. Payne, artist. Tennessee, 1872. Wood and paint. Height 19-1/2″, length 32″, width 8″. Photography by Bob Pennington. Tennessee State Museum.

page 124   **Fiddle.** Joe Henry Hundley, artist. Axton, Virginia, ca. 1920. "Queen of Sheba" fiddle; scrollhead carved in the shape of a lion. Photography by Larry Harwell. Moore collection.

page 125   *Left:* **Detail of a grave marker.** William Lydon, stonecutter. Maplewood cemetery, Mayfield, Kentucky. Installed in 1899 when Colonel Henry G. Wooldridge was buried. *Right, top:* **Tombstone for William Cummin.** Attributed to Christopher Foglesong, stonecutter. Presbyterian Old Stone Church, Lewisburg, West Virginia, ca. 1825. Photography by Monique Fong. Shenandoah History, Edinburg, Virginia. *Right, bottom:* **Headstone with tree-of-life symbol.** Laurence Krone, stonecutter. St. John's Lutheran Church Cemetery, Wythe County, Virginia, ca. 1810. Photography by Monique Fong. Shenandoah History, Edinburg, Virginia.

pages 126 and 127   **Fireplace crane.** Blacksmith unknown. Quihi (near Castroville), Texas, ca. 1850. From the home of the Alfred Boehle family. Forged iron. Height 28″, width 35-1/2″. Inscribed "FM sh MF sh ML sh." Photograph courtesy of the San Antonio Museum Association. Collection of Robert Quill Johnson, deceased 1980.

page 127   *Top:* **Trivet.** Artist unknown. Cast iron, ca. 1850. Found in Page County, Virginia. Photography by Larry Harwell. Moore collection. *Left:* **Andirons.** Found in Patrick County, Vir-

ginia, ca. 1900. Photography by Larry Harwell. Courtesy of Blue Ridge Institute/Ferrum College, Ferrum, Virginia. *Right:* **Shovel.** Artist unknown. Wrought iron, nineteenth century. Found in Shenandoah County, Virginia. Photography by Larry Harwell. Moore collection.

page 128   **Four graveyard crosses.** *From left to right:* Cross with abstract floral designs for the palms and a large iron heart above the crossing; wrought iron, ca. 1800–1850; height 39-1/2″, width 22-1/4″. Cross with fleur-de-lis palms and a heart of bent iron at the crossing; wrought iron, ca. 1790–1850; height 43-1/2″, width 30-1/4″. Cross with fleur-de-lis palms and brass bosses; wrought iron, ca. 1790–1850; height 42-1/4″, width 26″. Cross with diamond-shaped crossing and abstract floral designs for palms; wrought iron, ca. 1790–1850; height 36″, width 20-1/4″. All crosses: artists unknown. Louisiana State University Rural Life Museum, Baton Rouge, Louisiana.

page 129   **Two key baskets.** *Top:* Maker unknown. Leather. Chesterfield County, Virginia, ca. 1850. *Bottom:* Maker unknown. Leather with initials "R.F.H." tooled on both ends. Richmond, Virginia, ca. 1850. Both baskets: Photography by Katherine Wetzel. Courtesy of Dr. R. Lewis Wright.

page 130   *Bottom, left:* **Baptismal font stand.** Maker unknown. Possibly Hahira, Georgia, ca. 1875–1900. Southern yellow pine, jig-cut with original paint. Height 35″, width 34″, depth of top 29-1/4″. Photography by Michael McKelvey Photographer. Museum purchase with funds donated by the Decorative Arts Acquisition Trust, 1982.35. Permanent collection of the High Museum of Art, Atlanta, Georgia. *Top, left:* **Double or "courting" dulcimer.** Maker unknown. Found in northern Georgia. Dulcimer made for two people to play while seated facing one another. Photography by Larry Harwell. Moore collection. *Top, right:* **Bank.** Attributed to John George Schweinfurt. New Market, Virginia, mid-nineteenth century. Earthenware. Abby Aldrich Rockefeller Folk Art Center, Williamsburg, Virginia.

page 131   *Top, left:* **Crucifixion.** William Edmondson, artist. Limestone, ca. 1932–1937. Height 18″, width 11-7/8″, depth 6-1/4″. National Museum of American Art, Smithsonian Institution; gift of Elizabeth Gibbons-Hanson, 1981.141. *Top, right:* **Bible.** M. L. Sherman, artist, Confederate soldier. Carved stone with tintype fitted on cover. Height 5-3/4″, width 4-1/2″, depth 1-1/2″. Engraved front: "M.L. Sherman/ To my Wife K.S.E.S."; spine: "March 22, 1863"; back: "Taken from beneath Fort Robinette, Corinth, Miss." Collection of State Historical Museum, Mississippi Department of Archives and History. *Bottom, right:* **Chief Director of Mechanic Volunteer Fire Company No. 1, Louisville.** Artist unknown, ca. 1828. Polychromed wood. Height 78″. Collection of the J. B. Speed Art Museum, Louisville, Kentucky.

page 132   **Early photograph of Aberdeen and Rockford Engine No. 35.** Decorated with a silhouette Indian and full-bodied eagle, made in North Carolina. Print by Carlton Palmer. Photograph courtesy of Jean Lipman. Exhibited in *American Folk Art in Wood, Metal, and Stone,* by Jean Lipman. **Locomotive ornament.** (Similar to one in above photograph.) Artist unknown. Red and white paint on iron, ca. 1880–1900. Found in western Piedmont region, North Carolina. Photography by Larry Harwell. Moore collection.

page 133   **Decoys.** Mud goose (standing with neck bending down): artist unknown; unidentified wood and iron rods; nineteenth century; height 15″, length 22-1/2″, depth 5″. Canadian goose: artist unknown; Southern pine, nineteenth century; height 9-1/4″, length 22″, depth 7-1/4″. Mud goose (standing, neck erect): artist unknown; unidentified wood and iron rods; nineteenth century; height 24″, length 13″, depth 4″. Female mallard: artist unknown; cypress or Southern pine; nineteenth century; height 6-3/4″, length 16-1/2″, depth 6″.

Pair of blackjack ducks, each: artist unknown; unidentified wood; nineteenth century; height 4-3/4", length 8-3/4", width 3". Four miniature decoys (male and female mallard, male and female pintails), each: artist unknown; unidentified wood; early twentieth century; height 3-1/8", length 5-1/2", depth 2-1/8". Mud geese are unique to Louisiana. Louisiana State University Rural Life Museum, Baton Rouge, Louisiana.

page 134   **Safe.** Maker unknown. Greene County, Tennessee, ca. 1830–1860. Walnut and poplar. Height 47-1/2", width 48-1/2", depth 17-1/2". Photograph by permission of *The Magazine ANTIQUES*. Private collection.

page 135   **Pie safe.** Maker unknown. Tennessee, ca. 1840. Yellow pine and tin. Photography by Bob Pennington. Tennessee State Museum.

pages 136 and 137   **Huntboard:** maker unknown, North Carolina, ca. 1870. Yellow pine stencilled with a corncob with pineapple motif. Splashboard remains (rare with huntboards). Pottery from Edgefield area. Photography by Larry Harwell. Private collection.

page 138   **Baby basket or cradle.** White oak splits and oak legs. Found in mountains of northwestern North Carolina, near Boone, ca. 1900. Photography by Larry Harwell. Courtesy of Blue Ridge Institute/Ferrum College, Ferrum, Virginia.

page 139   **Blanket chest.** Adam Neff either painted or owned the chest. Western Maryland, 1791. Poplar and yellow pine. Painted with unusual *scraffito* decoration technique, base restored. Courtesy of the Museum of Early Southern Decorative Arts, Winston-Salem, North Carolina, acc. 2738.

page 140   **Desk.** Maker unknown. Walnut and tulip, probably North Carolina, 1808. Found in Wytheville, Virginia. Height 47-1/4", width 42", depth 20". Courtesy, The Henry Francis du Pont Winterthur Museum.

page 141   **Dower chest.** Probably made by a member of the Huddle–Spangler family. Wythe County, Virginia, ca. 1800. Paint decoration on poplar. Photography by Larry Harwell. Moore collection.

page 142   **Blanket chest.** Maker unknown. Eastern Shore of Virginia, ca. 1770. Yellow pine with original green and white paint. Height 24-3/4", width 56", depth 20". Colonial Williamsburg Photograph.

page 143   **Cupboard.** Orange and blue paint on yellow pine. Found in Haymaker Town, Botetourt County, Virginia, ca. 1820. Photography by Larry Harwell. Private collection.

page 144   **Cupboard.** Maker unknown. Attributed to Randolph County, Piedmont, North Carolina, 1780–1810. Painted yellow pine. Height 84-1/4", width 48-3/4" (at base) 50-1/4" (at cornice), depth 21-3/8" (at base) 15-1/4" (at cornice). Courtesy of the Museum of Early Southern Decorative Arts, Winston-Salem, North Carolina, acc. 2073-22.

page 145   **Slab.** Clarke or Madison County, Georgia, 1870–1880. Yellow pine and birch. Height 47-1/2", serving width 44", overall width 46", depth 21". Photograph by permission of *The Magazine ANTIQUES*. Private collection. Exhibited (1983) by the Atlanta Historical Society in *Neat Pieces: The Plain-Style Furniture of Nineteenth-Century Georgia.*

page 146   **Cupboard.** Maker unknown. Montgomery County, Alabama, ca. 1870. Poplar grain painted to look like yellow pine. Height 72", width 42-1/2", depth 14". Photography by Jim Bathie. Courtesy of the Landmarks Foundation of Montgomery, Alabama.

page 147   *Left:* **Chest of drawers.** W. D. Evans, maker. Kernersville, North Carolina. Dated December 23rd, 1861. Painted and decorated tulip poplar and yellow pine. Photography by Spottswood Studios, Mobile, Alabama. Courtesy of the Fine Arts Museum of the South at Mobile, Museum Purchase Fund, P78.01.02. *Right, top:* **Safe.** Maker unknown. Taylor County, Georgia, 1835–1850. Yellow pine. Height 82-5/8",

width 43-1/2" (body) 48-1/4" (cornice), depth 19-3/4" (body) 22" (cornice). Photograph courtesy of the Atlanta Historical Society. Courtesy of Mr. and Mrs. Collins Sullivan and Mrs. Robert Hodges. Exhibited (1983) by the Atlanta Historical Society in *Neat Pieces: The Plain-Style Furniture of Nineteenth-Century Georgia. Right, bottom:* **Chest.** Maker unknown. Chest with drawers, 1760–1790. Gray-and-white marbleizing. Width 49-5/8". Colonial Williamsburg Photograph.

page 148   *Left:* **Corner cabinet.** Original painting and graining. Colonial Williamsburg Photograph. *Right:* **Washstand.** Maker unknown. Found in Columbia Furnace area of Shenandoah County, Virginia, ca. 1830. Smoke-grained paint decoration on pine. Photography by Larry Harwell. Moore collection.

page 149   **Box.** Maker unknown. Found in Columbia Furnace area of Shenandoah County, Virginia, ca. 1830. Smoke-grain paint decoration on yellow pine. Photography by Larry Harwell. Moore collection.

page 150   *Top:* **Blanket chest.** Maker unknown. Piedmont (Charlotte area), North Carolina. Painted yellow pine. Height 30-1/4", width 44-1/2", depth 19-7/8". Courtesy of the Museum of Early Southern Decorative Arts, Winston-Salem, North Carolina, acc. 2888. *Middle:* **Chest.** Johannes Spitler, maker. Shenandoah Valley, Virginia, ca. 1800. Yellow pine with walnut battens on ends. Height 23-1/4", width 49", depth 22". Private collection. *Bottom:* **Blanket chest.** Floyd County, Virginia. Photograph courtesy Blue Ridge Institute/Ferrum College, Ferrum, Virginia. Owned by Blue Ridge Farm Museum, Ferrum College, Ferrum, Virginia.

page 151   *Top:* **Safe.** Found in Alexandria, Virginia, 1840–1860. Painted poplar and pine. Height 58", width 40", depth 17-1/2". Photograph by Richard Boyd Photography by permission of *The Magazine ANTIQUES*. Collection of Mike Johnson. *Bottom:* **Case clock.** Painted decoration attributed to Johannes Spitler. Shenandoah (now Page) County, Virginia, 1800. Painted yellow pine. Abby Aldrich Rockefeller Folk Art Center, Williamsburg, Virginia.

page 152   **Sideboard.** Maker unknown. Scott County, Virginia, ca. 1840–1860. Walnut and poplar with punched tin panels. Height 44-1/2", width 62", depth 17-1/2". Photograph by permission of *The Magazine ANTIQUES*. Collection of Carol Flieger.

page 153   **Twig furniture.** Table, chair, footstool. Maker unknown. Northern Appalachian or Shenandoah Mountain region; chair dated January, 1908. Mountain laurel or *Rhododendron* limbs and pine. Table height 25", length 22", depth 17"; chair height 32", width 15", depth 18"; stool height 7", width 13", depth 7". Photography by John O'Hagan. Courtesy of Randy and Lee Sewell.

page 154   *Top, left:* **Safe.** Clements family. Greene County, Georgia, ca. 1820. Photograph courtesy of Atlanta Historical Society. Courtesy of Dr. and Mrs. James T. Bryson, Washington, Georgia. Exhibited (1983) by the Atlanta Historical Society in *Neat Pieces: The Plain-style Furniture of Nineteenth-Century Georgia. Bottom, left:* **Mirror.** Found in Bulls Gap area of Hawkins County, Tennessee. Walnut frame, ca. 1800–1820. Photography by Larry Harwell. Moore collection. *Right:* **Safe.** Maker unknown. Wythe County, Virginia, ca. 1850. Yellow pine with punched tin panels of flowerpot-and-tulip motif. Photography by Larry Harwell. Private collection.

page 155   *Top:* **Chippendale desk and bookcase.** Walnut with light and dark wood inlays. Inscribed: "J. S. Moore/ Victoria, Virginia." "Handle with care." Height 90-5/8" (40-3/8" desk, 50-1/4" bookcase), width 42" (at base), depth 21-7/8" (at base). Private collection. Courtesy of the Museum of Early Southern Decorative Arts, Winston-Salem, North Carolina, research file S-2482. *Bottom:* **Table.** Eastern Virginia. Applied diamonds.

Photograph courtesy of the Blue Ridge Institute/Ferrum College, Ferrum, Virginia. Owned by Jack Ericson.

page 156   **Chair.** Walnut and yellow pine. Height 34-3/4", width 21". Courtesy of the Museum of Early Southern Decorative Arts, Winston-Salem, North Carolina, acc. 2026-87.

page 157   **Bed.** Attributed to W. D. Evans. Kernersville, North Carolina, ca. 1860. Poplar grained to resemble rosewood. Headboard close-up shows incised eagle. Photography by Courtland W. Richards. Courtesy of Bryding Adams Henley.

page 158   **Sofa.** Christofer Friderich Carl Steinhagen, maker. Anderson, Texas, 1860. Oak and pine. Height 42", width 84", depth 25". The University of Texas at Austin Winedale Historical Center.

page 159   *Left:* **Corner cupboard.** Yellow pine and sycamore. Height 57-1/2", width 35", depth 20". Won first prize in woodcarving competition in San Antonio International Exposition. Photograph courtesy of the San Antonio Museum Association. Courtesy of Dr. and Mrs. W. Corbett Holmgreen. *Right:* **Desk and bookcase.** Kentucky. Height 42-3/8" (bookcase), 41-3/4" (desk), width 39-7/8" (desk), depth 43" (desk) 20" (bookcase). Private collection. Courtesy of the Museum of Early Southern Decorative Arts, Winston-Salem, North Carolina, research file S-3203.

page 160   *Top:* **Chest.** Walnut with maple and cherry inlay. Hall County, Georgia, 1830–1850. Height 23-7/8", width 48", depth 16". Photograph by permission of *The Magazine ANTIQUES*. Courtesy of Paul and Sally Hawkins. Exhibited (1983) by the Atlanta Historical Society in *Neat Pieces: The Plain-Style Furniture of Nineteenth-Century, Georgia. Bottom:* **Corner cupboard.** Attributed to East Tennessee. Height 96-7/8", width 43" plus 2-3/4" at each corner. Private collection. Courtesy of the Museum of Early Southern Decorative Arts, Winston-Salem, North Carolina, research file S-13208.

page 161   **Miniature chest.** Walnut with light wood and cherry inlay. Height 16-3/8", width 17-5/16", depth 11-5/8". Courtesy of the Museum of Early Southern Decorative Arts, Winston-Salem, North Carolina, acc. 2500.

page 162   *Left:* **Chest.** Maker unknown. Inscribed: "Martha Johnson." Found in Polk County, North Carolina, 1820–1840. Yellow pine. **Candlesticks.** Stamped "Craven" pottery. Steeds, North Carolina, ca. 1900. Redware. **Fireboard** (above chest). Maker unknown. North Carolina, ca. 1850. Yellow pine. Painting of a coonhound or bluetick hound. Photography by Larry Harwell. Private collection. *Right:* **Table.** Maker unknown. Attributed to Tennessee, ca. 1850. Walnut with inlay of bellflower-type motif. Photography by Larry Harwell. Private collection.

page 163   **Huntboard.** Maker unknown. Spartanburg County, South Carolina, ca. 1830. Yellow pine with red-and-black sponge decoration. **Swan.** S. Williams, maker. Knotts Island, North Carolina, ca. 1982. Photography by Larry Harwell. Private collection.

page 164   **Virginia chest.** Signed "Godfrey Wilkin Hardy County and State of Virginia." Walnut with yellow pine, inlay probably sulfur, dated 1801. Inscription on end of chest: "Well don." Height 34-1/2", width 54-3/4", depth 26-1/2". Collections of Greenfield Village and the Henry Ford Museum, Dearborn, Michigan, negative no. B25500.

page 165   *Top:* **Case clock.** Inlaid decoration. Courtesy of the Museum of Early Southern Decorative Arts, Winston-Salem, North Carolina, acc. 3415. *Bottom:* **Chest.** Maker unknown. Mecklenburg County, Virginia, ca. 1800. Yellow pine and paint with cutout heart in apron. Photography by Larry Harwell. Private collection.

page 166   **Crazy Quilt.** Maker unknown. West central Georgia, 1889–1911. Velvet, silk, wool, other. 76" square. Photography by John O'Hagan. Courtesy of Randy and Lee Sewell.

Clock, Peter Rife.

Blanket chest, Tennessee.

Designed by Bob Nance

Mechanical art by Design for Publishing
Homewood, Alabama

Text type is Linotron 202 Trump Medieval by Akra Data, Inc.
Birmingham, Alabama

Color separations by Capitol Engraving Company
Nashville, Tennessee

Printed and bound by Kingsport Press, Inc.
Kingsport, Tennessee

Text sheets are Patina Matte by S.D. Warren Company
Boston, Massachusetts

*Endleaves are Elephant Hide by Process Materials
Corporation*
Carlstadt, New Jersey

Cover cloth is Kingston Natural Finish by Holliston Mills
Kingsport, Tennessee

Southern Folk Art is the latest of several exhibitions that Philip Morris has sponsored to draw attention to parts of our culture that have not received the recognition they deserve. We hope this exhibition will provide exciting discoveries about ourselves and our history for all Americans. Philip Morris is proud to be associated with this landmark exhibition.

Hamish Maxwell
Chairman and Chief Executive Officer
Philip Morris Incorporated